Tercentenary Esoteric Edition

PANTHEISTICON :
SECRETS OF ALL AGES FOR THE LEARNED
The Wizard's Handbook of John Toland

*A Modern Edition of the Mystical Classic
Hermetic Philosophy Society Handbook on
External and Internal Doctrines of the Ancients*

Revised & Enhanced
by
JOSHUA FREE
for
*The Mardukite Library Archives
& NexGen Systemology Society*

Originally Published in 1720.

NexGen Esoteric Library Archives Series
edited by Joshua Free

CYBERNOMICON
DELOMELANICON
DRACONOMICON
NECRONOMICON: ANUNNAKI BIBLE
PANTHEISTICON

NexGen Systemological Library Series
edited by Joshua Free

AWAKENING
REALITY ENGINEERING

Forthcoming by Joshua Free

THE BOOK OF PHERYLLT (*Kima Global Books)*

THE PANTHEISTICON OF JOHN TOLAND
Tercentenary 300th Anniversary Edition

Text Revision, Annotation Notes & Enhanced Design
© 2018, Joshua Free for the Mardukite Truth Seeker Press
in association with the NexGen Systemological Society

mardukite.com

PANTHEISTICON:

SECRETS OF ALL AGES FOR THE LEARNED

The Wizard's Handbook of John Toland

A Modern Edition of the Mystical Classic
Hermetic Philosophy Society Handbook

Revised & Enhanced
by
JOSHUA FREE

THE MOST FAMOUS DEPICTION OF JOHN TOLAND
(...and he is holding a copy of the *Pantheisticon*.)

TABLE OF CONTENTS

Humans consider themselves unique so they've rooted their whole theory of existence on their uniqueness. One is their unit of measure, but it's not. All social systems we've put into place are a mere sketch. One plus one equals two. That's all we've learned. But one plus one has never equaled two. There are, in fact, no numbers and no letters. We've codified our existence to bring it down to human size to make it comprehensible. We've created a scale so that we can forget its unfathomable scale.

– Lucy (2014)

FOREWORD

*"Gateways and doorways are for entrance and exit,
and we are justifiably annoyed when people stand
in them and talk. Perhaps that is the trouble with so
many of our Gateways to Truth. There is too much
talking in them, and too little getting through."*
– Gertrude Moakley (1959)

JOHN TOLAND coined the term "pantheism" in 1705, describing the philosophical paradigm of *Spinoza* – a doctrine that identifies "God" or *divinity* with the whole of the Universe – All-as-One. As revealed in the pages of the PANTHEISTICON, this Secret Doctrine, observing a "Universal Law" animating and acting upon all things, is actually one-to-one with an "*Esoteric*" *Truth* known among learned brotherhoods since ancient times – and it is not the same as the "*Exoteric*" truths vulgarly thrown about and debated on the surface world for the Realm of the masses.

PANTHEISM is named for a "divine energy" imbuing and encompassing All Things and the "Cosmic Law" that dictates the natures of All Things and their energetic interactions with each other. This Truth exists at all levels – those we can observe causally and even those we only see effects from. It exists independent of human belief and whims of fantasy, yet is responsible for sparking both. It was observed among elite classes of the ancient world just as it has been carried forth into modern "New Age" systems via mystic traditions of Freemasonry, Rosicrucians, Illuminati, and in the case of this *"wizard's handbook of John Toland"* – the founding father of Antiquarian NeoDruidism.

Other later noted public "subscribers" to this form of PANTHEISM include: Johann Wolfgang von Goethe, Georg Wilhelm Friedrick Hegel, Ludwig van Beethoven, Ralph Waldo Emerson, Alfred Lord Tennyson, Henry David Thoreau, Walt Whitman, Leo Tolstoy, Robert G. Ingersoll, Nikola Tesla, Carl Jung, Albert Einstein, D.H. Lawrence, Ansel Adams, Alan Watts and Timothy Leary (among countless others). All of these folk made vast intellectual contributions and demonstrated an understanding of the Universe that required going *beyond* or *outside* of what the external or societal (mass) capacity allows: hence since the days of the Ancient Mystery School, *"Esoteric Truth"* has remained for the most part "occult" – "hidden" in the folds of those meeting in *Societies* outside the boundaries of the Realm.

JOHN TOLAND published his PANTHEISTICON in 1720 (along with a related work CLIDOPHORUS excerpted in the appendix of this tercentenary 300th anniversary edition) with only a few copies circulating privately. In spite of the "Universal Truth" professed, in its time, the title, use of pagan ideology and a liturgy imitating that of the Church of England was as offensive as the appearance of a "Satanic Bible." The PANTHEISTICON is so relevant to NexGen Mardukite and Systemological paradigm studies that I prepared this annotated edition to the public from within our private Esoteric Library Archives.

My initial encounters with John Toland's work go back to the mid-1990's during my installment into the modern *"Pheryllt Druid"* tradition. During my apprenticeship, I studied *"antiquarian neodruidism,"* an intellectual period sparked by the posthumous release in 1726 of Toland's *"History of the Druids,"* or more specifically, *"History of the Celtic Religion & Learning, Containing an Account of the Druids,"* based on the letters commissioned by Lord Viscount Molesworth before Toland's death in 1722. Of his contributions to *druidism*, based on my original apprenticeship notes, I wrote in my *"Book of Druidry"* (2001), and since reprinted in *"The Druid Compleat"* anthology :

> "John Toland founded the first neo-druid Order in 1717: '*The British Circle of the Universal Bond*' [*"An Druidh Uileach Braithreaches"* (ADUB)], based on his own Celtic Researches. To some, the group is also known as ADO – the *"Ancient Druid Order."* Some of the *"mesopagan"* neo-druids, like Henry Hurle (a member of John Toland's ADO), viewed neodruidism as an extension, if not a purely Celtic equivalent to, Eurasian Freemasonry – also revived in England at the Apple Tree Tavern of Covent Garden in 1717."

In only three centuries passing, so much legend and controversy surrounds our history of the *antiquarian neodruidism* inception, evolution, and its direct link to the 1717 British revival of Freemasonry by the Premier Grand Lodge of England, that an entire digress thesis could be written regarding that alone.

Of his *esoteric* and *exoteric* legacy we can best summarize drawing from his own *epitaph*, which he composed a few days before his death:

> "Here lies JOHN TOLAND, born in Ireland, near Londonberry, who in his youth studied in Scotland, Ireland, and at Oxford: and, having repeatedly visited Germany, spent his manhood about London. He was a cultivator of every kind of Learning; and skilled in more than ten languages: the champion of Truth, and the assertor of Liberty, but the follower or client of none: nor was he ever swayed either by menaces or misfortunes, from pursuing the path, which he chalked out to himself, uniformly preferring his integrity to his interest. His Spirit is re-united to his heavenly Father, from whom it formerly proceeded; his Body yielding to Nature, is also re-placed in the Bosom of the Earth. He himself will undoubtedly arise to Eternal Life, but will never be the same *Toland*. Born 30th November, 1670. Seek the rest from his Writings."

And to his writings we shall seek the rest...

Enjoy the journey, dear Truth Seeker.

The Truth Against The World.

~ JOSHUA FREE
Lughnassadh 2018
"Mardukite Babylon"
San Luis Valley, Colorado

INTRODUCTION

TO THE LEARNED AND INGENIOUS READER
FROM JOHN TOLAND

———————

As one, who has the interest of mankind greatly at heart, and as a strict votary of the eternal Truth, I present to you, (candid reader) a *New Fellowship* and *New Regulation*; by the embrace of which, you shall not only become better and wiser, but even live a Life of Joy, a Life of Happiness and Contentment. By what chance, or care, these Things have been now brought to Light, it neither is my business to tell you, nor does it concern you to know. For to form a competent Judgment of them, our sole View must be directed towards themselves, we must even consult nothing but themselves, as no extrinsic estimation, much less authority, can enhance their Value.

The generality of mankind is averse from Knowledge, and vents invectives against its partisans; but as *Seneca* nobly instructs us: "To use our utmost efforts," however cattle-like, "we might not follow the herd of those that go before; going not where we should go, but where they go." And in a few lines after, "Since every man chooses to believe rather than judge, Life then is never brought to a scrutiny – Credulity has always the ascendant, error handed down from Father to Son embraces our Thoughts in its mazes, we give headlong into it: In a word, it is the dull infatuation of being led by the examples of others, that exposes us to ruin."

11

What therefore remains to be done? "We shall be in safety," says he, "if we separate ourselves from the Multitude; for the Multitude," as the same author inculcates a little after, "is a proof of what is worst." – and "nothing is so vulgar," in the opinion of *Tully*, "as to have no relish for Knowledge."

"Philosophy," to continue the use of *Tully*'s words, "contents itself with a few Judges; it designedly shuns the Multitude, as conscious of its jealousy and hatred; so that should one undertake to vilify and cast an odium upon Philosophy in general, he may do it with approbation of the people; or, should he strive to attack the Philosophy that we adhere to, he may find great resources in the systems of other Philosophers."

For your part, learned and ingenious Reader, if you choose to follow Reason, rather than Custom, for your guide, you shall repute all human casualties to be placed in a degree far beneath you; you shall, patiently take up with your lot, whatever it is; you shall keep foolish ambition and gnawing envy at a distance from you; you shall despise perishable honors, being to perish yourself in a short time; you shall lead a peaceable and pleasant Life, neither admiring nor dreading any Thing; and you shall deservedly apply to yourself these *Verses of Virgil* –

Felix qui potuit rerum cognoscere causas,
Atque metus omnes & inexorabile fatum
Subjecit pedibus, strepitumque Acherontis avari.

Blessed be the Man!
Who could of Things the secret Causes trace;
And cast all Fears, and Fate's unmoved decree,
And roaring Acheron, beneath his feet.

Be such by reading this PANTHEISTICON – And when you know that it is a Philosophical, and not a Theological discourse, that is here given of the society, (for there is a wide difference between unfolding Nature's Mysteries, and discoursing on religion) I shall bid you be wise, and farewell.

MARDUKITE

THE ANCIENT AND MODERN
SOCIETIES OF THE LEARNED
&
A DISCOURSE ON THE INFINITE
AND EXTERNAL UNIVERSE

I.

Man, as a social animal, can neither live well, nor happy, not at any rate, without the help and concurrence of others; therefore several societies, nay innumerable societies, necessarily arose from the very nature of the Thing. Husbands enter into a strict alliance with wives, parents with children, masters with servants, magistrates with subjects, and finally, from the coming together of all those men, with their respective families, the union of living in cities is formed. Some of these societies are more voluntary, others less. The former, of which we speak here, were called by the ancient *Greeks* and *Romans – Brotherhoods, Friendships, Fellowships, Societies.* The latter too, affect very often the same appellation; but we are not to treat here of the *corporations* of merchants and artisans, nor of religious *communities*, and political *assemblies*; such were the *Arval Brethren, Titian Companions, Augustals, Flavials* and *Antoniniani.*

What we speak of here are those societies that were frequently instituted among the *Greeks* and *Romans*, either for the pleasure or instruction of the Mind.

Religious assemblies, especially if held in the night-time, and all others, either running upon politics, or interesting themselves in any shape with regard to the Commonwealth,[1] were often restrained and prohibited by the laws; as also those solemn *regalios*, many of which were celebrated on stated Days of the Year, to say nothing of the Companies of Artificer Masons,[2] that are vastly different from ours. This misfortune, or disgrace, seldom or ever befell learned Fraternities, friendly and facetious banquets, which were called by the Greeks, *symposia*[3] and *syndeipna*, and by the Latins, *compotationes* and *concenationes*,[4] not unlike the *sussitia* of the Spartans.

Each member of the society contributed something towards the supper, that was to be in common; this contribution was called by the Greeks, *symbolum* or *symbola*; and by the Romans, to use *Cicero*'s term, *collecta*, from which the entertainment itself was called, *caena collatitia*; those who contributed nothing were *asymboli*, *i.e* scot-free. The *symbolum* moreover was called by the Greeks, *Eranium*, the supper *eranos*, the guests *eranifiae*, and the master of the feast *eranarcha*.

---

1 *Commonwealth* – the "Realm" or world of the public masses, the people of the nation or state as a collective identity.
2 Presumably "Masonic" fraternities, including Druids and Rosicrucians, &tc.
3 *Symposium* – an assembly meeting or conference for the discussion of some Thing, particularly where multiple persons are addressing the assembly in turn; else a conversation held after a dinner. From the Greek *symposion*, meaning "drinking together."
4 Terms indicating communal eating and drinking mealtime customs.

II.

But as nothing in Nature is more beautiful than disposition and order, so, in all such banquets, the
Brethren, who, for the most part, should not be
more in number than the muses, nor fewer than the
graces, or rather the exact number of the planets,
chooses among themselves, by casting the dice, a
President, who might point out for them the Order of
Drinking and Argument.[5]

This *President*[6] was also characterized with several
Titles, as the *Manager of the Club*, the *Chief*, the *Umpire*, the *King*, the *Captain-General*, the *Father of the
Supper*, the *Lord of the Banquet*, the *Master of the Rev-
els*, according to *Cicero*; and, according to *Varro*, the
Steward of the Feast. For which reason, *Jupiter Good-
fellow*[7] was worshiped under that Name, as the most
equitable Mediator and Arbitrator of the Laws of social life.

Whoever is willing to know the qualities that are a
requisite for a good *President*, must consult at leisure
the fourth question of the first book of *Plutarch's*

---

5 The customs and rituals to be observed by the society or
   fellowship.
6 *President* – as used within the text of a society meeting, the
   person responsible for *presiding* over the *Form* (the general
   order and rites of the *society*), in this case as given in the body
   of the *Pantheisticon*.
7 Jovian energy current and personification: Greek, *Zeus*; Latin,
   Dys Pater or *"Jupiter"* as heights of the Planetary
   ("Olympian") pantheon. The original Mesopotamian inception
   suggests a position of *father* or *Lord* of the "local" Solar-
   System.

Symposia, for they regard rather the Laws of Drinking and Argument. Now as these banquets were seasonable or unseasonable, more or less delicate and sumptuous, those which *Hermogenes* calls, *Socratic Entertainments,* easily bore the sway over all others, and were justly more commendable. We have a specimen of them in the writings of the two most excellent disciples of the divine *Socrates,* to wit, *Plato* and *Zenophon.*

III.

Our age likewise has produced not a few, who, at table, desirous to dispute freely, and with less restraint, upon any topic whatsoever, instituted Entertainments, not unlike those of the *Socratics,* and even called them, not improperly, *Socratic Societies.* Most of these are Philosophers, or, at least, in a degree bordering upon Philosophers: bigoted to no one's opinion, nor led aside by education or custom, nor subservient to the religion and laws of their country; they freely and impartially, in the silence of all prejudices, and with the greatest sedateness of the Mind, discuss and bring to a scrutiny all Things, as well sacred (as the saying is) and profane.

These *Philosophers* are called, for the most part, *Pantheists,* upon account of an opinion concerning GOD and the UNIVERSE, peculiar to themselves; but diametrically opposite to the *Epicureans, Chaologists,* and *Oneiropolists,* as they acknowledge no first Confusion, no Fortune, much less Chance, to be the Maker of the World. Notwithstanding they deliver their sentiments, concerning the cause and origin of Things, in conjunction with *Linus*, the most ancient, most authentic, and revered Oracle of mysterious science, saying:[8]

> *All Things are from the Whole,*
> *and the Whole is from all Things.*

This short sentence, which they always have in their mouth, requires to be fully explained, wherefore we shall here briefly clear it up, by adjusting exactly Words to Things.

They assert that the Universe (of which this World we behold with our eyes is but a small portion) is Infinite both in extension and virtue, but One, in the continuation of the Whole, and contiguity of the parts: immoveable according to the Whole, as beyond it there's no place or space, but moveable according to the parts, or by distances in number infinite:[9] incorruptible and necessary both ways, to wit, eternal in existence and duration: Intelligent also by an eminent Reason, and not to receive its denomination from our intellectual faculty, unless by a slight similitude: Finally, whose integral parts are always the same, and constituent parts always in motion.

---

8   "All Things are from the All, and the All is from all Things." (As from the original Greek rendering.)

9   "One continuous spectrum of wholeness differing only in degree as perceived parts." (As explained in the NexGen Systemology book, *Reality Engineering* by Joshua Free.)

I could not express these Things in so concise a manner, with greater perspicuity, yet for the further satisfaction of the reader, I shall animadvert upon them, one after another.

IV.

From that Motion[10] and Intellect that constitute the Force and Harmony of the infinite Whole, innumerable species[11] of Things arise, every individual of which is both a Matter and Form to itself, Form being nothing else than a disposition of parts in each body. From whence therefore we may conclude, that the best Reason and most perfect Order, regulate all Things in the *Universe*, in which there are infinite Worlds, distinguished from one another, as other Parts by their peculiar Attributes, although, with regard to the Whole, there are no Parts really separate.[12]

Things moving by Parts in no wise take away from the Perfection of the *Universe*, as thereby new Perfections are produced, by a never-ceasing Principle of Generation. Neither is the constant dissolution of

---

10 "Motion" – the specific function, movement, manifestation or condensation of energy according to its nature and interactions with other natures.

11 "Species" – the word used by John Toland to denote inorganic variation of "type."

12 "All is One. There is nothing separate; no parts or levels, except as distinguished by the mind, which fragments Wholeness into separate parts." (A main tenet of NexGen Systemology work established by Joshua Free.)

many Things, that result from those parts,[13] a hindrance to its Perfection, inasmuch as this is a Point of the greatest Perfection; for nothing of the Whole perishes, but destruction and production succeed each other by turns,[14] and all by a perceptual change of Forms, and a certain most beautiful variety and vicissitude of Things, operate necessarily towards the participation, good, and preservation of the Whole, and make, as it were, an everlasting circulation.[15]

That celebrated 'Darling of the Muses' was of Opinion, *That from One all Things are made, and shall be reunited to the same.*[16] Finally, the Force and Energy of the Whole, the Creator and Ruler of All, and always tending to the best end, is GOD, whom you may call the *Mind*, if you please, and *Soul* of the *Universe*;[17] and hence it is, that the *Socratic Brethren*, by a peculiar term, as I said before, are called PANTHEISTS; this Force,[18] according to them, being not separated from the *Universe* itself, but by a distinction of Reason alone.

---

13 Things that "grow together from those parts."
14 The "ebb and flow" of all Things within a Wholeness of consistency.
15 Recurssion or the Recursive Spiral. (As it is defined in NexGen Systemology.)
16 "Out of One all Things sprung, and are to be dissolved into, and confounded with, the same again."
17 God is defined as "the (systematic) Mind and (energetic) Soul of the Universe."
18 The Universal Agent, a permeating (cosmic) energetic singularity of All.

Gregory of Ariminum, *Occhamus*, *Cajetanus*, *Thomas Aquinas* even (who was canonized), to name only a few, thought this philosophy did not contradict the 'Mosaic Formation of the World' (and neither do I), when they taught, *That God was the eternal Cause of the eternal World, and that all Things, from all Eternity, flowed from God without a Medium*; but *Jerom* thinks finely upon the Matter, when he says, *That God is infused and circumfused, both within and without the World*. And this is the sentiment of the ancient Philosophers, especially of the *Pythagorics*.

V.

To set still, in a clearer Light, the manner of the PAN-THEIST'S philosophizing, I say, that the first Bodies, or the Elements (if I am allowed the expression of the Elements) are most simple, and actually indivisible, infinite too in number and species,[19] and that all Things are made out of their composition, separation, and various mixture, but with proper measures, weights and motions; to wit, with a mutual and mechanic proportion and disproportion of parts in their nature moveable, and with a mutual determination of concurring and impelling Bodies, which without any Void are divided into their own Elements.

There is no "intermission of determinations" inasmuch as there is no Space void and vacuum, nor a

---

19 Variation, degree, type or frequency being distinguished from a singular continuous spectrum. (As defined in *Reality Engineering* by Joshua Free.)

last Barrier. *There's no such Thing as a progress of motion in infinitum* – as there are infinite individual "points" where neither a First nor a Last can be fixed upon; and so we grant there is no infinite determination, or any particular species of motion; yet, at the same time, we make no allowance for a first corporeal moveable, or an immovable Center of the *Universe*, or even a *Center of the Universe* in any sense whatsoever.[20]

As to the devices of *Epicurus*, who asserted, that Things were cemented, and concreted together, by rough and smooth, and hooked and crooked Bodies (not forgetting the interposition of his Void), we shall leave them to himself, with his fortuitous "Concourse of Atoms" and declination of the same not extrinsically determined; acting, perhaps, something in his distances between diverse Worlds; that we should not dwell long upon the eternal "descent of atoms to a line," and such parallels, when in an infinite Space, neither the highest nor the lowest, nor the middle nor the last, can be conceived.

Internal and universal action, the chiefest of all motions, is circumscribed by no limits, the *Universe* itself being unlimited, wherefore there will be no absurdity in establishing an infinite action; but all particular motions mutually terminate, refrain, retard, or accelerate themselves, according to the manner and strength of every resistance or im-

---

20 Hence quantifiable measurement of all Things defined as *time* and/or *space* is "relative" when contrasted against an *Infinitude* with no "absolute" definitions (determinations).

pulse.[21] Our design does not permit us to dispute here, either upon the mutual action of the Globes[22] against themselves, or upon arguments in defense of a Void, which have been advanced by Philosophers of no small repute. Whoever feeds his fancy with these notions, let him consult *Newton*.[23]

In compounded Bodies[24] are contained, as we said, Particles of every species, that cannot be cut or parted,[25] this or that species having the ascendant, for

---

21 Forces and energies in the Universe follow a course and interact based on their natures (and design) as if set in a definitive motion with infinite varying degrees of possibility.

22 "Globes" as the spherical fields occupying space as energy particles (or vibrations) and molecular substances.

23 Newtonian Physics dominated the higher intellectual scientific world during John Toland's lifetime, (similar to the scientific monographs of the Rosicrucians and Freemasons) hundreds of years before the era of Einstein, Quantum Physics and String Theory – all of which are more recently incorporated into metaphysical pursuits. Toland does not discredit physical sciences; his work is simply intended to relay a philosophical or mystical (or conceptual) "working understanding" of the *Cosmic Universe* where these other "calculations" are simply deemed "unnecessary" for current purposes.

24 Referring again to the spectrum of manifestation as "elements" – core materials to include all visible and invisible "stuff" existing in the *Universe*. This is particularly evident in all aspects related to the electromagnetic (EM) spectrum – a singular continuous force that is perceived as a myriad of "elements" from heat, to x-rays, to audible sound, to physical light, &tc.

25 The original belief of the "Atomist" Philosophers being that the "atom" is effectively the smallest particle of existence. Atoms are now named for this ancient mystical belief from Greece even if they are semantically not the 'smallest components' of material existence. This misnomer erupts from the fact that all physical and natural sciences evolved or

(according to the old maxim) – *the more there is in a Thing of the substance of another, the more it will derive from it its appellation*; so that, it comes to pass, that there's no real innovation in the World, except the sole "Permutation of Place,"[26] from which proceed the "production and destruction of all Things," as such, by generation, increase, alteration, and such like Motions. For all Things, as we already remarked, are in Motion, and all diversities whatsoever are so many names for particular Motions, not one single point in nature being absolutely at rest, but only with regard to other Things,[27] rest itself being truly and essentially a "Motion of Resistance."

VI.

Thought, which we must not omit speaking of, is a peculiar motion of the Brain, the proper organ of this faculty; or rather a certain part of the brain continued in the Spinal Marrow,[28] and in the nerves with their membranes,[29] constitutes the primary

---

developed from older mystical and philosophical schools, even borrowing from the vocabulary.

26 *Permutation* – a change in arrangement (or re-arrangement) of parts within a set; mathematically, the rearrangement does not change the total value of the set, only its variables and variable positions; for example, *abc, bca, cba,* &tc.

27 Everything is connected together. There are no "Things" existing in exclusion to other "Things."

28 "Spinal Marrow" – spinal "column" that begins in the brain and runs along the ridge of the back.

29 "*Meninx,* a thin membrane which encloses the brain, whereof there are two, the one thicker called *dura mater,* the other thinner, called *pia mater.*" (From the original notes to the 1751 edition.)

"Seat of the Soul," and performs the motion both of thought and sensation; which vary wonderfully, according to the different structure of the brain, in all kinds of animals. As to other movements of the body, performed by means of the nerves, we will not undertake to speak of them here.[30]

The Ethereal Fire[31] environing all Things, and therefore supreme; permeating all Things, and therefore intimate, of which a kitchen fire is a certain analogical and imperfect similitude; the Ether, I say, by a wonderful structure of the Brain thereunto adjusted, and by exterior Objects that act on the Brain, through the means of the nerves of the senses, and excite therein various imaginations,[32] duly executes all the machinery of conception, imagination, memory, amplification and diminution of Ideas. It is this Fire alone, more fleeting than Thought itself, and by far more subtle than any other kind of matter, which can with so quick a motion run over the tended Cords and Ligaments[33] of the Nerves, and variously agitate them, according to the different "impressions of objects" upon the Nerves.

---

30 The paradigms and vocabulary structures of anatomy, physiology and biology are not being deemed obsolete, but the semantics and natures described by them are outside the specific scope of this metaphysical discourse.

31 Although semantically rejected by contemporary science, the "Ether" is a mystical equivalent to the modern concept of a "unified field" or "universal stream of consciousness."

32 The process by which external stimuli (perceived data) is conceptualized internally as our conscious experience of "Reality."

33 "Filaments and threads" of the Nerve system. (From the original notes to the 1751 edition.)

The Ether is a reviving Fire, infusing a sweet and gentle warmth, not burning, not dissipating, not consuming as ordinary fire. *It rules all Things, it disposes of all Things, according to Nature, without noise, and imperceptible, either to the sight or touch. In it is soul, mind, prudence, increase, motion, diminution, alteration, sleep, watching, it governs All in all Things, and never allows celestial and terrestrial Beings to be at rest.* This Fire is *Horace*'s "Particle of Divine Breath,"[34] and *Virgil*'s "inwardly nourishing Spirit," of heavenly origin and fiery vigor.

Now by what means imaginations are excited, or Ideas formed in the Brain (an organ, although very complex, is corporeal and can produce nothing but what is corporeal) we made to appear in our second book *Of Esoterics*,[35] where we demonstrated that all Ideas whatsoever are corporeal. Rejecting the notions of some, who figure to themselves that the diaphragm is the "Seat of the Soul," or the heart, or liver, or other parts; "It behooves one to know," (says *Hippocrates*, or rather *Democritus*, in that valuable "Treatise upon the Falling Sickness") "that no other part but the brain affords us pleasures, as mirth, laughter, diversion; and, on the other hand, grief, anxiety, sadness, and mourning: By its means

---

34 The "Divine Spark" in NexGen 'Mardukite' and 'Systemological' metaphysical literature.

35 Referencing the anthology *Tetradymus* by John Toland, from which the second book is titled: *Clidophorus*, or of the Exoteric and Esoteric Philosophy, that is, of the external and internal doctrine of the ancients: the one open and public, accommodated to popular opinion and established religions; the other private and secret, wherein, to the few capable and discrete, was taught the real Truth stripped of all disguises.

we become wise, and understand, and see, and hear, and know what is safe and honest, good and bad, agreeable and disagreeable, discerning some of them by rule, and perceiving others by the advantage that is annexed to them: By the same, in their proper times, we distinguish pleasures from what are not so, and the same Things please us not always: By the same we grow delirious and run mad, we nurse terrors and fears, some haunting us by night, others by day, our Thoughts are taken up with dreams, we give into unseasonable errors, er are possessed by empty cares, we are ignorant of standers-by, and we fall into a disuse and forgetfulness of Things. All this is occasioned by the brain, when it is not in its due position; that is to say, when it is not sound, but is hotter or colder, moister or dryer, or in fine, experiences any Thing contrary to what is natural or usual."

VII.

The Seeds of all Things, begun from an eternal Time, are composed out of the first bodies, or most simple principles,[36] the four commonly received Elements[37] being neither simple nor sufficient: For in an Infinity all Things are infinite, nay even eternal, as nothing could be made out of nothing, and therefore we may conclude, that the organic "Structure of Seeds"[38] could not be itself formed out of any "con-

---

36 The first form, first movement or progression of the All-as-One into "motions" creating existence from a basic form.

37 The classical or alchemical elements: *earth, air, fire* and *water.*

38 The "Seed of Life" or matrix-program (encoded design) that

course of atoms" or any species of motion whatsoever.

To illustrate this tenet by some example or other,
the Seed of a Tree is not alone in "Power"[39] a Tree,
according to the notion of *Aristotle*; but a real Tree,
in which are contained all the integral parts of a
tree, though so minute as not to be perceived[40] by
the senses without microscopes, and not even then,
but in a very few Things. All that this Tree wants is a
fuller "distinction and magnitude of parts," which is
gradually acquired by the application of simple bodies[41] of distinct species, that are, as so many
constituent parts, necessary to the "nourishment
and increase" of that simple body.

Following this example, no species of trees perishes,
in as much as the seeds, in which it lives, always remain alive, and should they be received in a proper
place, forthwith they imbibe a more distinct con-
formation, nutrition, augmentation, and by degrees
arrive at a due Perfection.[42] The same may be said of

---

determines the possible energetic natures and interactive
motions of manifestation.

39 The "Seed" is *potentia*, capable of becoming a Tree, or in a
possibility of being a Tree.

40 The "fractal-like" pattern (encoded design) for the Whole (or
All) is found in its entirety within the most minute
distinguished "part" suggesting that the total pattern for the
whole and all parts (for all things) operates All-as-One.

41 Growth and accelerated progression through duplication and
expansion following the same encoded program.

42 "For primitive beings like us, life seems to have only one
purpose: gaining time. And it is going through time that seems
to be also the only real purpose of each of the cells in our
bodies. To achieve that aim, the mass of cells that make up

the other species of the *Universe*, not only of animals and trees, but also of stones, minerals, and metals, which are not less vegetable and organic, having their own Seeds, formed in their own Matrix, and increasing with a particular specific nutrient, as well as men, quadrupeds, reptiles, birds, fishes, and plants.

VIII.

It is true: Philosophers are for the most part of the opinion that gold, crystal, &tc. are familiar, or bodies of like nature and parts, made up of an external apposition, or any other way, because they appear so to the senses. But the *Pantheists* think, that they consist of dissimilar parts, from whose comprehension, (this, or that having the ascendant, as a "principle of composition") arises the body called *Homaeomeres*.[43] There is no such Thing to be met with as a similar mixed body, not even in metals and stones, for chemists demonstrate, that such bodies are cemented by a manifold growing together of

---

human beings has only two solutions: be immortal, or to reproduce. If its habitat is not sufficiently favorable or nurturing, the cell will choose immortality. In other words, self-sufficiency and self-management. On the other hand, if the habitat is favorable, they will choose to reproduce. That way, when they die, they hand down essential information and knowledge to the next cell. Which hands it down to the next cell and so on. Thus knowledge and learning are handed down through time." (Quoting 'Professor Norman' in the movie *Lucy*.)

43 "*Homeomeria*" as in the likeness of parts.

several substances;[44] from gold, that which nothings seems to be more similar, they extract sulfur, quicksilver, Earth and other Things, that go into the composition of this noble metal (though not all Things, as this would exceed the bounds of human industry).[45]

In stones and metals we may behold sundry shapes of veins, such as the shoots, as it were, of branches and roots, spread far and wide, which they have in their mines and quarries; from which, (to appropriate to myself the words of a certain philosopher) a friendly aliment gently filtrates,[46] first through passages more lax, afterward gradually through more narrow ones, to refine and make purer the nutriment, and finally, an exhalation passes through thin and hidden pores. As the blood flows up and down, and is driven to the extremities of the body, so in the nature of blood an alimentary substance distills through the narrow holes of stones and metals, where each part, through its own Conduit, sucks in what is befitting its nature.

---

44 Chemistry now further demonstrates that altering the condensation or concentration of electron energy (perceived to us as "quantity" of electrons) moving about a Thing changes the ("specific") nature of the thing and its interactions ("motions").

45 Possibly an allusion to the physical alchemists craft attempts toward the "Philosopher's Stone" or "White Powder" that is reputed to transmute the "species" composition and type of all Things to "gold."

46 *Prolecta / Prolectatur* – "from whence, by an attractive charm, or by way of a lure, &tc., the genuine significance of the Word." (From the original notes to the 1751 edition.)

If such an analogous nutritious "sap" is less percept-
ible in them, than in the stomach and veins of
animals, let him remember, who requires this from
Nature, that a distinct aliment from the parts does
not appear more Trees than in something else,
whose anatomy, notwithstanding, has been executed
by several. If one should say, that in plants there are
found certain figures of a trunk, branches, leaves,
blossoms, fruit, seeds, than so also in these all this
may be found, either analogous, or in a different
manner:[47] And as plants themselves do not shrub
after the same way, why then should we admire, if
Things propagated under the Earth, meet with a different Kind of Life?

The one who at any time observed innumerable
gems, beautifully distinguished by various figures, to
grow in certain places, there's no reason he should
believe, they were less actuated with Life, than the
teeth and bones of animals.[48] As every country is not

---

47 Although more easily understood as an example, the analogy
of the Tree – its seed, programmed growth (encoded
progression), all facets of its possible nature, &tc. are
contained within each part – this analogy applies to all Things
in existence equally, even if not as readily apparent in the
mind.

48 Such doctrines proliferated by John Toland throughout the
discourse are semantically more representative of the
philosophical (or mystical) belief called *animism*, far more
than *pantheism*, by traditional definition. *Animism* is a
paradigm whereby a "spiritual essence" or "supernatural
power" *animates* the foundations of the material and *Universe*
– non-human entities such as animals, planets and other
inanimate "Things" carry a "Divine Spark" that codifies and
defines their nature and interaction with other natures.
Pantheism is defined as a more generalized concept whereby

productive in every Thing, in like manner, all stones, and all plants do not grow everywhere; every place does not afford a proper nourishment to every particular. Hence, marble grows here, diamond there; one stone puts on its due form sooner, another stone later; this seed generates pebbles, that one rocks. Stones receive an increase and decrease, are more or less durable, as well as all other vegetative beings. But some are at a standstill when they perceive no room for nourishment and increase through such hard bodies, and such narrow pores.

Who (say they) can believe that the vast bulks of stones and metals are nourished like bones, and increase by vegetation? What nutritious Force can soften and dilate that invincible hardness? But (to answer them by another question) what is admirable here, that we behold not also in the teeth and bones of animals? They are harder than most stones and metals, notwithstanding they imbibe their aliment through minute and imperceptible conduits, and increase according to every dimension. Yet that teeth may receive the addition of a new substance, it is necessary that each part should be as firmly compacted, and diffused into a larger bulk, which in like manner would be feasible, if a tooth was equal to a mountain or island.

If this is no matter of wonder with regard to bones, and the hardest trunks of trees, why then, should it

---

all manifestations in the *Universe* are representative and energetically linked to the same "God" appearing manifold throughout the pattern of *Creation* ("Seed of Life"/"Matrix of the Universe") or unified field.

seem next to a prodigy with regard to stones and metals? As growing Trees and Trees hewed down differ, so stones in quarries, and stones hewed out of them: Those are alive, and these are dead; those in their native beds are full of "sap" and these torn asunder are destitute of moisture, and at length are reduced to dust. In a word, every Thing in the Earth is organic, and there is no equivocal generation, or without its own Seed, of any Thing in Nature.

It is not without reason, that the Earth should receive the appellation of "Mother" – Panspermia,[49] to whom the Sun - Pammestor[50] is a never decaying "Husband"; and this justifies my answer to a German innkeeper, who impertinently importuned me to tell him what countryman I was? *The Sun is my Father, the Earth is my Mother, the World's my Country, and all Humans are my Relations.* As if an ignorant and insipid person should accost me with this verse out of Homer – "Who? From whence are you? Where's you city? Where were you born?"

IX.

The Pantheists maintain the Pythagoric Astronomy, more properly called the Egyptian, or to speak in modern terms, the Copernican - placing the Sun in the center of the planets that turn about it,[51] among

---

49 *Panspermia* – "A Mixture of all Seeds" (From the original notes to the 1751 edition.)

50 *Pammestor* – "A Master, that influences all Things." (From the original notes to the 1751 edition.)

51 This "heliocentric" paradigm is also evident in the ancient

which our Earth is neither the least nor the most in-considerable: Like unto it, there are other innumerable Earths, making their revolutions in stated times, according to their own respective dis-tances about their own Suns, or Fixed Stars, as they are often called.[52] The same they steadfastly hold to, with regard to comets that describe the greatest ob-served circles. Good Gods! While they devote themselves to the study of surveying the Heavens and the Earth, what an exquisite pleasure arises from the everlasting courses of wandering Stars?

In the contemplation of these courses they calculate both the velocity of the lesser and slowness of the greater, actuated with one and the same motion of Nature.[53] Hence, they easily conclude that there are no real wanderings of the planets, none of them ret-

---

Mesopotamian renderings of the *Sumerians* and *Babylonians* that paralleled and in many ways even predated and contributed to the *Egyptian* methodology. As time and culture developed, classical philosophy and sciences of the *Greeks* and later *Romans* evolved from what remained from the Golden Age of long-lost *Egyptians* and *Mesopotamians*.

52 The overall worldview presented by John Toland as *Pantheism* does not discredit or discount the possibility of other "living worlds" (Earths) operating elsewhere in the *Universe*, following with the singular fractal-like spread of existence we can observe. These observations self-honestly lead us to believe that the same operative "Motions" taking place on a *Universal Level* are in effect taking place everywhere, and at all levels, in accordance to its own "specific nature." That the organic and intelligent "Life" on "Earth" should somehow be an anomaly or exception to the greater infinite *Universal Pattern* (or "Seed") is highly unlikely.

53 Applying the subjective human perception of "earth-time" in which to calculate the course of all heavenly bodies.

rogrades,[54] none of them stands still, none of them goes out of its right pathway, no matter how these particulars might appear to the eyes of men. They also known exactly in what sense ancient connoisseurs understood the "Music of the Spheres" – *That so great and so sweet a Sound*, says Cicero, *joined together by unequal rests, though in the exactest proportion, is the result of the impulse and motion of the Orbs themselves, and mingling sharps with flats, constantly produces several harmonious concerts.*

The more ancient and wiser kind of philosophers understood this, not of distinguishing a flat or sharp sound, not of the seven-fold division and agreement of tones, but of the wonderful harmony of these Motions;[55] while poets departing not from their art, indulged their fancy, and while the monstrous forgers of solid spheres grew delirious, and as a punishment for their folly, in a manner heard the rapidity of the sound. How many and what agreeable problems are easily solved by the pupils of the *Pantheists!*

As among other Things, by what means the slowest star can get up to the quickest, which is not alleged here, as a Thing difficult to be explained, but that, in a few words, I might give some hints of their doc-

---

54 Retrograde is only a perception from the viewpoint of the Earth while it goes about its own motions in relation to other planetary bodies.

55 The key aspect to the 'Celestial' matters is that the planets each and all together represent "vibration" and "frequency" as we distinguish their types and also as they harmoniously interact together as a "system."

trine, with regard to the the "Co-Incidence of Extremes" (if I am allowed the term), seeing that, pursuant to the Rules of their Institutes, I am not allowed to lay open the Whole.

X.

From this "Co-Incidence of Extremes," the PANTHE-ISTS deduce a certain Third, and truly wonderful Motion of the Earth; which is to be measured by the "Progress of the Equinoctial Points" and therefore, by the slow, but continued declination of the meridian line.[56] The "Axis of the Earth," I say, rolls without ceasing, always parallel to itself, around the pole of the ecliptic, from which it is distant in every place, twenty-three degrees and a half, inclining to the plane of ecliptic, and the equinoxes by degrees proceed to the southern parts, having nothing to do with the ecliptic. There can be no clearer demonstration than this, founded upon the observations of *Aristarchus, Eudoxus, Hipparchus, Ptolomy, Copernicus, Halley*, and other excellent ancient and modern astronomers.

When the Equinoxes come to the Tropic of Capricorn, there is a necessity of their proceeding farther to the Antarctic Pole, and so afterward by turning about the Arctic. *We Britons* in reality are more remote now from the Arctic Pole, than in the time of *Pytheas* the *Massilian*: Although the eighth sphere[57] is

56 Toland is describing the movement of the Earth's axis and "Precession of the Equinoxes."
57 Eighth Sphere – the "Celestial Sphere" or "horizon" of fixed

at so great a distance from the Earth, that the diversities, magnitudes, and oppositions of the celestial appearances, described by ancient astronomers, seem not to have so much changed to the senses, throughout the course of two thousand years and upwards;[58] but that we have in effect come nearer to the Antarctic Pole, not only the seasons of the year, little by little altered by the progress of the Equinoxes, are a testimony; but also a milder temperateness of the same seasons, all which evidently appears from history and the authority of observations.

This third motion (which I call Equinoctial, to distinguish it from the diurnal and annual motion of the Earth) proceeding gradually from East to West, brings matters to to pass, that the sphere, called the eighth, or the region of visible fixed stars, though immoveable, might seem, nevertheless, to go from West to East; so that whether the eighth sphere moves over the poles of the ecliptic in *consequentia*,

---

star constellations beyond the "wandering spheres" of the "seven planets." The constellations of the "zodiac" appear in this sphere or field of space immediately surrounding our relative view of the physical *Universe* as seen from the Earth.

58 Precession causes an era-shift in "Celestial Age" approximately every 2,160 years. Each "Celestial Age" is marked by observation of a 30-degree arc of the full 360-degree celestial horizon – of which there are twelve (30 x 12 = 360). A specific fixed constellation appears in each of the twelve 30-degree arcs of view (as seen from the Earth) and these compose the "signs" of the "zodiac" in contemporary astrological astronomy. The relative position of the Sun and Earth in proportion to the celestial horizon on the Spring Equinox is what determines our "Celestial Age" – which is currently Pisces and will eventually be Aquarius.

or whether there is a "Progress of the Equinoxes" in *antecedentia*,[59] the appearances will be the same, and all the same Things will affect our sight. This phenomenon should be explained the same way, as the other motions of the Earth, formerly attributed to the Sun and planets, and it must be rescued from the absurdities of prating cavilers, both which we have sufficiently acquitted ourselves of, in the book of *Esoterics*.

XI.

As a natural consequence of this equinoctial motion, every particle of our globe, and the same may be said of the other planets, must, in the course of the ages, undergo all sorts of adventures and vicissitudes. *This inclination*, says every *Pantheist, shows that the axis of the Earth does not always pass through opposite parts. When it comes to pass, that little by little, and insensibly different regions, are placed under the axis, and the inhabitants of the zone, now frigid, are brought back and turned to the equinoctial line; and, at length, the place of the arctic pole to the antarctic, and the east to the west, which* Herodotus, *from the sacred authority and mysterious monuments of the Egyptian priests, testifies to have happened formerly twice.*[60]

---

59 *Consequentia* and *antecedentia* – whether or not such a Thing is the *consequence of* or has *come before*, the visible result may be unchanged.

60 A phenomenon called "axis mutatis" in esoteric and mystical lore.

That is to say, the Sun has twice before entered a period to set where it now rises, and rises as often where it now sets. This has happened, not only twice, but also innumerable times, and will happen again in the eternal duration of Things, although such a conversion of the stars, and a reduction of all parts into the same situation, requires a revocation of about thirty-six thousand years.[61] *Capernicus*, it seems, would fain reduce this number to twenty-five thousand years.

But from this observation, (as that most ingenious man proceeds) on which mathematicians should employ all their care and study, we perceive a singular understanding of Nature and admirable providence, that the same part of the Earth should not be condemned to so long a cold, but that each, and every region, might partake in its time, of all the aspects of the Sun; which, notwithstanding, upon account of the slowness of motion, and the short life of man is not discerned.

That change of the axis might be also a proof of the force, whereby the Earth directs itself to a certain part of the eighth sphere, to pass gradually from one to another place of the Earth; whence there is a necessity of the climates of regions being changed, and the latitudes of cities, and the situation of sun-dials placed upon the Meridian Line.

---

61 Each of the twelve 30-degree arcs of the "Celestial Sphere" requires 2,160 earth-years to pass through. This means a complete procession or "revolution" through the entire cycle would require 2,160 x 12 (or 25,920) earth-years. The 36.000 year cycle estimation was a misunderstood calculation derived from sacred Mesopotamian mathematics which is sexagesimal (base-60) – for example why we divide an hour into 60 minutes or a wheel into 360 degrees.

Moreover, the Equinoctial Line of the Earth is changed with the axis, and passes to another part of the Earth; but as it is always perpendicular to the axis, if no other change happened, the Equinoctial Line would be still found under the Star of Aries,[62] *as it was in the Time of* Eudoxus, *and the Equinoctial Points would not have moved forward in antecedentia.*

Notwithstanding, that this comes to pass, it is most certain, for now the largest star in the horn of *Aries* (in which, in *Eudoxus*'s time, the vernal equinox was placed) with regard to the ecliptic, has at least the breadth of three degrees toward *Pisces*; but with regard to the equator it has such a bending, that it almost touches the Tropic of *Cancer*. Wherefore it necessarily follows, that the ecliptic is changed, which was in the time of *Eudoxus*.

XII.

The same change, by an almost parallel reason, holds good with regard to fluids and solids, moisture

---

62 When traditional astrology is set down from 2160 B.C. through the Chaldean Dynasty of Babylon during the 6-7th centuries B.C., the axis point of the Equinoctial Line correlated to the constellation of Aries (in the eighth sphere or Celestial Sphere) and thus is known as the "Age of Aries" for which the first month of the year, corresponding to the Mesopotamian New Year festival of Akiti (Akitu or Zagmuk) at the Spring Equinox, corresponded to the sign of Aries and is thus given as the birth-sign of Aries for those born March 21 through April 20, &tc. Given equinoctial precession, people born today during this period are technically no longer actually born under that observed sign.

and dryness; for whatever is sea now, was formerly
land, and all that is now land, will, in time to come,
be sea, the bulk and aspect of the *terraqueous* globe
remaining always the same. This is a new doctrine I
confess, but a very true one; and of this opinion, unless I am mistaken, was, among other disciples of the
Egyptians, the *Clazomenian Anaxagoras*, who asked,
whether the mountains of *Lampsacum* were to be at
any time sea? Yes, says he, *unless time should fail*. For
he believed, that they were partly discovered, and
partly made by the ebbing of the sea, (as we shall explain elsewhere)[63] and that they should be
overwhelmed and consumed by its flowing.

Whereas the ocean, not without reason, was called
by the ancients *amphitrite*, because it environs, tears,
and makes a havoc of the Earth. The slowness of
these conversions carries a face of difficulty, when
observed by some of the Learned; but it is by those
who proceed slowly: Whereas, if the observations
are made by the more sprightly, most commonly
they become neglected by all, if not eventually entirely forgotten.

Hence it is that Theophrastus *dying*, (according to the
relation of *Tully*) *is said to have accused Nature, for
having granted a long life to harts and ravens, that did
not want it; and such a span to men, to whom it would be
of vast consequence to live longer; and could their days be
lengthened, all arts and sciences would be brought to a
perfection, and man's life would be improved in all kinds
of learning. He, therefore, complained, that Death seized*

---

63 Explained in the following section (XIII).

him, when he had just began to have a glimmering Light of these Things.

We examine not how justified this complaint is, neither do we deny the truth of *Hippocrates*'s maxim – *Life is short, but Art is long*. However, we are not entirely destitute of all help to pass a judgment upon the Equinoctial Motion, as it is evident to the Learned, that the same points of the Earth turn no more toward the *Great Bear*, the *Lesser Bear*,[64] and other fixed stars, which in the time of *Hipparcus*, or even of *Ptolemy*, had such a situation,[65] to say nothing of the remarkable changes of shores, islands, and other parts of our globe, occasioned by this vicissitude. Far be it from be, that I should assert any thing, that is not proved by experience and reason, it is therefore why I reject every precarious hypothesis and empty conjecture, which are denied with a better right than projected. I discard, in like manner, and pass the same impartial judgment upon Things granted, and not evident or proved, and all such fallacies, on which very often lies the whole stress of a *demonstration*.

---

64 "Or the star in the tail of the *Lesser Bear*." (From the original notes to the 1751 edition.)

65 An observation of ancient astronomy and "celestial magic" throughout the ages, suggests that a shift in the northern horizon or polar stars has shifted from *Thuban* (the Dragon, *Draconis*) and *Polaris* (the Great Bear, *Ursa Major*) and that this shift also is evident in the ceremonies and rites where thousands of years ago, cults viewed the *Draco* constellation as a primordial gate, which eventually shifted to the *Northern Dipper* with the circulation of the *Great Bear* around a central point. However they may have been interpreted, noted changes and observation of these "Great Cycles" in the cosmos was clearly significant and important to the ancient Learned.

XIII.

By this ebbing or declination of the sea, I spoke of (which we allow to be more easily proved from the long continuance of time, than from observation) certain bodies can be fully accounted for, especially sea-bodies, which are found in every part of the Earth, and not only buried deeply, but also very often broken from huge rocks, and the hardest marble.[66] Also that much of these rocks are the real and identical bones, spoils, remains of fishes, and other animals,[67] the learned *Woodward*, after the attempts of some others, has copiously demonstrated, a man of great depth in these studies, and deserving well of the learned World for his curious observations, and for showing that these are not sports of nature, nor stones of their own kind, but terrestrial fishes or shells, as many others have idly dreamed.

For all species of stones (as we hinted previously) receive their increase, as well as all other organic plant-life, from a loose fluid matter suitable to them, which matter sometimes shuts up within itself the hard and small bodies that perchance fall in its way, or running into such bodies, if hollow, and by degrees petrifying therein, as in a Matrix, finally assumes their form.[68] Thus is it, that we must like-

---

66 The Earth is mainly land encased in water with portions of land at times falling either above or below the general *sea-level*. There is a water-level beneath mostly all "dry-land" as well, such as is drawn from wells. Also there are places where water "springs" forth, such as certain mountainous locales.

67 Fossils discovered on "dry land" that are suggestive of ancient "water-beds" otherwise occupying.

68 The distribution of minerals and nutrients required for growth

wise explain the origin of figured stones, as the *Ech-ites*,[69] and *Conchites*,[70] and all of the like kind. *Esoteric Philosophers* furnish us with a ready explanation; but not the universal deluge, such, as there never was, the globe of the Earth still remaining, nor that ever it could in reality be effected by the separation of parts, whatever way any one should take to explain it.

I say this, was a due deference to the learning and reputation of *Burnet, Woodward, Whiston*, and others, who have not exactly understood the narrative, or dived thoroughly into the design of that wise law-give *Moses*, with regard to the origin of things, and the general flood;[71] not to say that the history his-tory of this *Egyptian Philosopher* concerning the rise, fall, and immediate vicissitudes of Things, abridged afterward by those that followed him, was supersti-tiously wrested from its genuine significance by

---

of all organic Things (including stones) and also the distribution of the like in an another manner for the calcification and petrification of the same Things.

69 "A precious stone of a darkish green colour and somewhat like a vapor." (From the original notes to the 1751 edition.)

70 *Conch* – "stones, I suppose, formed from the shells of fishes, and resembling pearls." (From the original notes to the 1751 edition.)

71 To say nothing regarding what other cultures have written of concerning such events, or more specifically, the accounts found on the most ancient cuneiform tablets of Mesopotamia (Sumerians and Babylonians) who illiterating such events in the origins of the current civilization established (or re-established) after the "flood" in Mesopotamia and Egypt – all of which centered around a "higher class" of being called "Anunnaki" in Mesopotamian languages.

many, or vastly corrupted by idle jugglers.[72]

As the figuration of stones is understood by the *Pantheists*, so also are the representations of plants, and other Things impressed upon stones; but trees dug out of heathy grounds and marshy places, are deservedly for most attributed by them to tempests, inundations, earthquakes, and to folk who have hewed them down, which I myself have very often found cut and burnt:[73] This is evinced from proper arguments, that cannot be now alleged; for we must not here go to the bottom of Things, or defend to particulars. Upon these (before recited) most solidly laid foundations of the immense and eternal *Universe*, the *Pantheists* build their philosophy, and embellish it with all possible perfections. A more subtle explanation of Things, and the solutions of phenomenons are to be within our discourse on *Esoterics*,[74] it being our design presently to write historically and not physically.

---

72 The oldest account of a "deluge/flood disaster" comes from Mesopotamian (Sumerian and Babylonian) cuneiform tablets which describe a period where this cyclic shift of the Earth was a natural occurrence, albeit foreseen by the "Anunnaki" figures. They selectively informed leading members of their own devotees concerning preparations for their survival and the survival of key elements of the world (called the "arts of civilization"). From this knowledge, which the Egyptians equally could account for, the Judeo-Semitic and later Christian lore of "Noah's Ark" emerged.

73 "Burnt and scorched towards the root as the bog (Fir) found in *Ireland*." (From the original notes to the 1751 edition.)

74 *"Clidophorus: Exoteric and Esoteric Philosophy."*

XIV.

It will not be amiss to remark, as we go along, that the excellent author, earlier quoted (whom I judge to be not *Hippocrates*, but some one more ancient) delivered in a few words, like so many oracles, the whole "Doctrine of the Revolution of all Things," and appearances remaining always the same. For after having reasoned upon the primary Elements of Nature, together with their infinite concretions and secretions, and deduced accurately from them this theorem:

Every Thing is to All, as All is to every Thing, he pursues his argument in the following words, as if delivered from a tripod: *Each, and every Thing, as well divine as human, is turned up and down; Days and Nights have their increase and decrease, so also has the Moon; there's an access of Fire and Water;*[75] *the Sun too has various appearances, with regard to us. Again, these and not these: Light to Jupiter is Darkness to Pluto, and Light to Pluto is Darkness to Jupiter. Those come to, and are transposed here, these there, in all Times. Those pass over what belongs to these, and these what belongs to those; they know not what they do, but they seem to themselves to know what they do, and what they see they know not; but all*

---

75 "That is to say, according to the right, oblique or parallel position of the globe, it appears longer or shorter over the horizon, or that by solstices and equinoxes, it produces the vicissitudes of seasons, and all other changes that happen in our globe. Whether this be a reasonable interpretation of the words given must be left to the determination of the ingenious reader, as the translator confesses he could not fathom, to his satisfaction, the meaning of them." (From the original notes to the 1751 edition.)

Things are actuated in them by a Divine Necessity, both what they will and what they nil. Now those coming here, and these there, and mingled though one another, every one of them satisfies its destined Fate, as well to more as to less.

When once we know, that in this remarkable passage by *divine* celestial bodies, are understood, and by *human* terrestrial, that *Pluto* signifies the centre of the Earth, or of every globe, and *Jupiter* the surface, or circumfused air: These, I say, being well understood, that humans will easily conceive all the rest, who, together with the mutual access and recess of *moist* and *dry*, or the sea and land, comprehends those Things I already inculcated, concerning the continued declination of the Meridian Line, and consequently, concerning the not less continued, though almost imperceptible change of the axis of the *Earth*. All these particulars duly considered, either with regard to the variation of particles always changing their place, or with regard to the constancy of never varying appearances, the condition of all the globes in the infinite *Ether*, is alike; the contemplation of which, is undoubtedly, not only the most agreeable, but also the most noble of all the Things that come within the verge of *true philosophy*.

XV.

That the abettors of the *Universal Deluge*, and general conflagration,[76] should not complain, that nothing is granted them; weighing Things in the scales of *Heraclitus*, and using his form of expression, we give up them what they desire, and yet we do not. We say, that the whole Earth was overwhelmed by waters, and it was not; and again, that all waters shall be conquered by fire, and shall not; but that no preposterous interpretation should be given to what we say, as it happened to that great philosopher, though upon a different matter, we shall set forth more manifestly our sentiments.

Wherefore we maintain, that, in reality, there's no part of the earth, but was some time or other covered by sea, and that there is no part of the sea, but will be, at length, possessed by the Earth;[77] for *dryness* very often, among the writings of the ancients, has the signification of *Fire*, of which it is both the property and effect. In the so often quoted books upon *Diet*, we several times meet with *Fire*, in the sense of *dry* or *solid*, it being usual with writers to put the effect for the cause.[78] The most ancient of

---

76 *Conflagration* – a large a destructive fire; literally "to burn up."

77 Denoted in apocalyptic prophecies as "land and sea trading places" or that the entirety of the Earth is not covered in water all at once but has an ebb and flow relationship on terrain, by its nature, ever in motion, as is the *cosmos*. In this elemental description, the moisture of water is polarized to the dryness of fire.

78 Ancient writings on *Diet* – writings of Babylon, Egypt and Pythagoras suggest the use of diet to balance the body for

the *Hebrews*, without any addition, used *dry* for *Earth*, and the most ancient *Greeks*, used *moist*, absolutely for *sea*. So also did *Moses* speak, so *Homer*. As therefore there is an access of *dry*, so also there is a recess of *moist*, interchangeably succeeding each other, as well in a macrocosm as microcosm.

The whole Earth, I say, was formerly buried under water, and the whole sea hereafter shall grow dry, or which is the same, shall turn to *Fire*.[79] From which places misconstrued, and from the mysterious words of the *Chaldeans* misunderstood,[80] flowed the prodigy

---

healing and health. All food and drink types are given qualities to correct imbalances, as divided by the elements: *sanguine* (*air* – hot and moist); *choleric* (*fire* – hot an dry); *phlegmatic* (*water* – cold and moist); and, *melancholic* (*earth* – cold and dry). Overproductive or underproductive elemental conditions in the body that result as ailments or illness may then be treated with the correct substances so as to bring an equilibrium. As such, the moistening, drying, heating and cooling of substances will also affect the reception of this materials or "nutrients" into the body.

79 It may be that in the cosmological development of the *Earth planet*, that the waters once covered the lands and were separated over time, given tides by the *Moon* and held in place by the *atmosphere* and *fields* of our unique planet. We can see from other planets that may have once possessed some similarity to our own that the collapse of *fields* and *atmosphere* and other calamities and changes in its cosmic past have turned these once *moist* water-bearing planets (globes, celestial bodies, &tc.) into *dry* desert badlands.

80 *Chaldeans* – the dynasty of the neo-Babylonian empire at its heights under King Nebuchadnezzar II, during which the key aspects of the cuneiform tablet mystical tradition were preserved, including the cosmological epic (the *Enuma Elis*) that the book of *Genesis* is based on, in addition to (the *Atra-Hasis* and) other tablets revealing the oldest accounts of the creation of man ("Eden") and the deluge ("Noah's Ark") that

of the *universal and final conflagration*. Now that any such thing, as that either an absolute sway of *moist* over *dry*, or *dry* over *moist*, has ever universally been, or shall be, in one and the same time, or together, as it is said, and at once; we not only simply deny it, but we prove that it is by no means possible. We are not so silly as to credit *Deucalionean* fables, and *Stoical* dreams, neither do we allow the supposed qualities of the *Peripatetics*, which generating like ones to themselves, can some time or other reduce, or change, all others into themselves.

Two theories are made out of these qualities,[81] upon the permutation of the Four Elements, as mixed, or, if they are simple, they are in no ways a fit, as we before remarked, to expound the varieties of Things,[82] as neither is the matter of *Descarte*'s first, second and third elements. Nature opens a more ready way.

Infinite, simple, and dissimilar substances, or the primary bodies of infinite species,[83] moveable and indivisible, make all the mixtures of all Things, of which they themselves are the eternal, exhausted,

---

our modern simplifications are all based upon. Detailed accounts of this information appear in the *"Necronomicon Anunnaki Bible"* edited by Joshua Free (now in its 10th Anniversary, Seventh Edition).

81 "Or rather the *Peripatetics*, by the means of these qualities, have botched up two theories upon, &tc." (From the original notes to the 1751 edition.)

82 All Things are an "alchemical" composition of basic elements based on their own unique nature and interactions with other Things and their natures. In such we see "energetic transference" and the motion of changing states.

83 *Species* – "specification" or "type."

and immutable matter. But the concretions, that proceed from this, as they have no other production than the various conjunctions of those bodies, so they have no other destruction than the separation of these same bodies, by whatever cause this falls out to be so. Thus it should not be apprehended that generation should at any time fail, the first substances remaining incorrupt, and there being always an assent and dissent of parts; neither, in like manner, is it to be dreaded, that any contrariety, whatever finally it is, should convert into itself, or consume the other parts of the *Universe*, as there can be no division, much less permutation of the first bodies. Hence chemists, alas! may despond of ever finding the Philosopher's Stone.

Therefore a constant and perpetual reciprocation of all possible mixed bodies follows, by which nothing is truly destroyed in the *Universe*; but, as I above mentioned, every Thing changes only its place; for which reason, though a creation out of nothing is looked upon, by the *Hebrew* Cabalists, and the philosophers of other nations, to be the production of a Thing, both out of the Nothing of itself, and out of the Nothing of a pre-existing Subject, yet all Things can be said to be properly *created*; for all Things, as we have shown, are so moved, as to make appear that there is a process and recess *in Infinitum*: And although the series of motions, and the series of all Things is eternal, yet there is no motion, no Thing eternal, but all Things are made anew, all Things are truly created. But of this elsewhere, now what follows.

XVI.

Inasmuch as (to return now into the Circle) Philosophy is divided by the *Pantheists*, as well as other ancient sages, into *External*, or popular and depraved; and *Internal*, or pure and genuine;[84] no discord arises among them, if every one of the *Brotherhood* professes the heresy he sucked in with his milk, (so it be not entirely false) or that, which has been any where established. They never enter into a dispute upon scholastic baubles, supposing that, in *indifferent matters*, nothing is more prudent than the old saying – *We must talk with the People, and think with the Philosophers*.

But should the religion derived from one's father, or enforced by the laws, be wholly, or in some respects, wicked, villainous, obscene, tyrannical, or depriving humans of their liberty, in such case the *Brethren* may with all the legality of the world, betake themselves immediately to one more mild, more pure, and more free.[85] They not only steadfastly assert and

84 Elsewhere Toland uses the terms "exoteric" (external, public) and "esoteric" (internal, secret, *Hermetic*, &tc.) to denote the division of philosophy (meaning "knowledge").

85 Let the wise and learned, the mystics and magicians, remain separate from the world in its ways. Should the time come – and it seems to be always eminently upon us – there must be a retreat in order to preserve the knowledge for the next generations outside the boundaries of the "realm" and in secret when necessary. In may very well be the case that the highest minds and beings (such as the "Anunnaki" in Mesopotamia, or the "Pheryllt" of pre-Druidic Wales) somehow separate from the masses at the inception of even this present version of civilization, were themselves the wise and learned of a former age and place, escaping from some other world set on disaster.

hold to a liberty of thought, but also of action, detesting, at the same time, all licentiousness, and are sword enemies of all tyrants, whether despotic monarchs, or domineering nobles, or factious mob-leaders.[86] Many of them are to be met with in *Paris*, in *Venice* also, in all the cities of *Holland*, and especially *Amsterdam*, and some (which is surprising) in the very court of *Rome*, but particularly and above all other place, they abound in *London*, and have placed there, as it were, the Citadel of their sect. It is obvious, I speak not of the *Royal British Society*, nor of the *French Academy*, nor of any such public assembly.

The PANTHEISTS, as I intimated, instituted moderate and honest banquets, not luxurious or scandalous, not to please a nice and delicate palate, but to bring together friends in *fellowship*, and relish the sweets of conversation. There is no carousing in their society, no gaming at hazard or dice, no piping, dancing, singing, stage-player entertainments, or farcical buffooneries. Instead: learned discourses, and app-

---

There is evidence all around the world showing these higher minds, may have at distant points, established refuges far and removed from the masses, to preserve knowledge and themselves.

86 The wise and learned, those remaining and gathering within the Realm, often elect to maintain membership in societies and organizations operating within the Realm and yet also removed. Within these societies – some such as are better recognized as Rosicrucian, Antiquarian Druidism or Freemasonry – the *esoteric* knowledge may be entertained and discussed among the learned who then take that with them back into the greater Realm. That these men should also partake in personal business dealings and worldly arrangements behind closed doors is the subject of much controversy and conspiracy in the present age.

ropriate jokes, and their operas and sweetmeats. These suppers, in a word, are not *Apician,*[87] or gluttonous, but pure, simple, and elegant: The table is frugal, though neat, and the brow often cheerful, but never lowering. Towards the end, the waiters and servants, as so many profane and illiterate persons, are shut out, and the doors being closely bolted, according to the customs of the ancients, the *Brethren* variously converse upon various topics.

As the bottle is in common to all, so also is discourse. Some question or other, besides the arguments perhaps started, is proposed to be solved by the Assembly, as in the *Platonic Banquet*: Or, as in the *Zenophontic* each person gives an account of his task, either imposed upon him by himself, or by others. They treat of serious and grave Things without contention, of ludicrous and pleasant, without levity: important disputes are entered upon, concerning the knowledge of the most worthy Things, and from matters indifferent aside agreeable interludes.

XVII.

As to the order that is observed in these Societies, they have a *President*, whose authority is the same as that which was formerly enjoyed by the *Greeks* and *Romans*, upon a like occasion. At every meeting the *Brethren* of every respective place are present, unless

---

87 *Apicius* – "an Epicure, who wrote a volume of ways and means to provoke appetite, spent a large estate on his stomach, and growing poor and despised, hanged himself." (From the original notes to the 1751 edition.)

some or other of them is detained by sickness, or is upon a journey, or can allege a reasonable excuse for absenting himself. They have, which most worthy to be related and known, *A Form of celebrating the Socratic Society*, divided into three parts, and containing the Laws, Axioms, and Maxims of the Society. We shall soon present the reader with a view of it. One part I always read in every meeting, the first usually, or the last, the *President* solemnly reciting before, the rest answering, and sometimes bearing chorus with him. Most is said alternatively, according to that verse of *Virgil*, *Homer* first suggesting it – *In alternative measures sing; Alternative measures please the Muses best.*

The whole *Form* is repeated on Solstices and Equinoxes, whose conversions, by the meditation and influence of the Sun, produces the vicissitudes of seasons, and all other changes that happen in our globe. The whole *Form* is also read at other times, especially upon the admission of a new *Brother*, which is never done but by the unanimous consent of all, although he can be discarded by a majority of votes. The *Presidents*, to make no room for debates in elections, follow the Order of their admission into the society, and in meeting the late *President* speaks first, and the new one is the steward of the feast. They frequently interpret the *Philosophical Canon*, which is placed in the Second Part of the *Form*, from which they deduce from it the most abstruse theorems of Natural Philosophy according to the sentiments of the ancient *Socratics*: And it is not amiss, that it is adjusted to the sentiments of the modern *Socratics*, to wit, the PANTHEISTS, or their

Brethren, as appears from propositions placed on the margin, that none should make the least scruple upon any particular, to pass by in silence (as I consult brevity) other interpretations of sublime matters made by them.

At stated times, they ruminate on the Law of Nature, that true and never deceiving *Reason*, (as it is exhibited in the last/third part of the *Form*) by the Brightness of whole Rays they dispel all Darkness, exempt themselves from trifling cares, reject all pretended revelations, (for what man of sense doubts of true ones) explode forged miracles, unreasonable mysteries, ambiguous oracles, and lay open all deceits, tricks, fallacies, frauds, old wives tales, whereby a thick cloud envelops *religion*, and a pitchy night overspreads *Truth*.

But the *Form* now presents itself...

MARDUKITE

THE FIRST PART OF THE FORM
(OF CELEBRATING THE SOCRATIC-SOCIETY)

THE MORALS AND AXIOMS OF THE SOCIETY

The PRESIDENT speaks.
May all happiness await our meeting.

The rest RESPOND.
We institute a *Socratic Society*.[88]

PRESIDENT.
May philosophy flourish.

RESPONDENT.
And the politer[89] arts.

PRESIDENT.
Attend with Silence.
Let this assembly, and all that is to be thought,
spoke, and done therein, be consecrated to Truth,
Liberty and Health; the triple Wise of the Wise.

RESPONDENT.
Both now and for evermore.

---

88 "We open this assembly/fellowship/lodge of the Nth degree,
&tc."
89 *Politer* – "courtly, refined, civil, gracious" (root = "polite").

PRESIDENT.
Let us be called Equals and Brothers.

RESPONDENT.
Companions too, and Friends.

PRESIDENT.
Let us banish Strife, Envy and Obstinacy.[90]

RESPONDENT.
Let us harbor Sweetness, Knowledge and Politeness.

PRESIDENT.
Let Jokes and Mirth be our pleasures.

RESPONDENT.
May the Muses and Graces be propitious.

PRESIDENT.
We must not be bigoted to any one's opinion.

RESPONDENT.
No, not even to that of *Socrates* himself:
And let us detest all *Priest-craft*.

PRESIDENT.
To make all Things, notwithstanding, the more
authentic, by the sanction of the proper authors,
and the best of humans, (without intruding though,
at the same time, upon the Rights of Liberty)
hearken unto, beloved companions, the words of the
most grave Censor *Marcus Porcius Cato*, related by

---

90 *Obstinance* – "refusing to change one's perception in spite of
contrary proofs."

Marcus Tullius Cicero, that renowned father of his country, in the thirteenth chapter of the book *De Senectute*.

RESPONDENT.
We are therefore Votaries of Truth and Liberty, that we might rescue ourselves from Tyranny and Superstition.

PRESIDENT.
"I always had," says Cato, "the greatest veneration for companions, and it was therefore, in my questorship, that I instituted Fellowships on the Annual Festivals of the *Great Mother*. I feast with my companions, but very soberly, as still there remained a certain heat of age, which gradually cooling, every thing daily became more mild and temperate. Moreover, I esteem not so much feasting for the pleasure of the body, as for the coming together and conversation of Friends. Our ancestors justly called the sitting down of friends at table an *Entertainment*, because it tended to the cementing of social Life: The *Greeks* who call it *Drinking* and *Supping together*,[91] have not termed it so well, inasmuch as, in that respect, they seem to make the greatest account of what should be made the least."[92]

RESPONDENT.
Let *Socrates* and *Plato* be praised,

---

91 See Prologue Section I, concerning the *Greek "symposium."*
92 The purpose of the "Feast" or "Festival" gathering *is* the "gathering" or "Fellowship" itself and not a matter of the grandiose nature of the meal itself.

And *Marcus Cato*, and *Marcus Cicero*.[93]

PRESIDENT.
Let us discuss every Thing seriously, and fill up the Charms of Discourse with diverting stories.

RESPONDENT.
Wittily, modestly, facetiously.

PRESIDENT.
Let us search out, diligently, the Causes of Things, that we might live pleasantly, and die peaceably.

RESPONDENT.
That free from all Fear, neither elated by joy, nor depressed by sadness, we might always maintain an unshaken constancy.[94]

PRESIDENT.
That we may also laugh to scorn the bugbears of the silly people, and the inventions of the crafty knaves, let us sing an *Ennian* strain.

PRES. & RESP.
"I value not a straw of the Augur *Marcus*,
Nor strolling quacks, nor strolling fortune-tellers,
Nor soothsayers, nor dream-expounders:

---

93 The function and "Form" of the *Pantheisticon* is in the philosophical stylings of classical (*Greek*, &tc.) philosophy, although the patina could easily be changed to fit other appropriations.

94 *Stoic/Stoicism* – a school of philosophy founded by Zeno of Citium, maintaining that "the wise should be free from passion, unmoved by joy or grief, and submissive to natural law."

They are all an ignorant Pack of Boobies,
Superstitious prophets, shameless conjurers,
Idle, crazy, poor vagrants – What they themselves
Have no faith in, others forsooth must believe;
From those, they promise riches to, they crave a
groat,[95]
Let them, then, from these riches subtract the groat,
And restore the remainder."

PRESIDENT.
Hear still to (ye best of Friends) the same wise *Cato*,
in the fourteenth chapter of the same book, *De
Senectute*, teaching as divinely after his example.

RESPONDENT.
To be healthful, cheerful and happy.

PRESIDENT.
"I take a singular pleasure," says he, "in the
magisterys that have been instituted by our
predecessors; and in the *discourses* that, according to
ancient *custom*, are made by the *Steward of the Feast;*
and in the cups, as in *Zenophon's* banquet, although
small, yet bedewed with liquor; and in a cooling
arbour in the summer, and in the grateful
vicissitude of the Sun's warmth, and that of a winter
fire. These pleasures of life I also seek after, in my
Sabine retirement, and constantly make one of the
guests at the entertainments of my neighbors, which
we spin out till it is late in the night, discoursing
upon various topics."

---

95 *Groat* – a silver coin used in medieval Europe (worth about
four pence).

RESPONDENT.
Let *Zenophon* by the theme of our praise;
And the rustic *Sabines*, the subject of our imitation.

PRESIDENT.
Let us greatly feed our Minds;
But sparingly our bellies.

RESPONDENT.
'Tis just, and good.

PRESIDENT.
Let us toast the Graces.

RESPONDENT.
Come, 'tis a sober toast; and we shall drink it
soberly.

THE SECOND PART OF THE FORM
(OF CELEBRATING THE SOCRATIC-SOCIETY)

THE DEITY AND PHILOSOPHY OF THE SOCIETY

PRESIDENT.
Keep out the profane people.

REPONDENT.
The coast is clear, the doors are shut. All's safe.[96]

PRESIDENT.
All Things in the World are one,
And one is All in all Things.

RESPONDENT.
What is All is all Things is God,
Eternal and Immense,
Neither begotten, nor ever to perish.

PRESIDENT.
In him we live, we move, and exist.

RESPONDENT.
Every Thing is sprung from him,
And shall be reunited to him,

---

96 After the mealtime has been completed, any of the servants,
caterers, &tc. who are attendants but not "installed" (initiated)
into the *Society* are dismissed from the lodge and the doors are
locked.

He himself being the Beginning,
and End of all Things.

PRESIDENT.
Let us sing a hymn,
Upon the Nature of the *Universe*.

PRES. & RESP.
"Whatever This is, it animates all Things,
Forms, nourishes, increases, creates;
Buries, and takes into itself all Things:
And the Same, of all Things is the Parent;
From thence all Things, that receive a Being,
Into the same are anew resolved."

(*Sometimes adding the following.*)

"All Things within the Verge of mortal laws
Are changed – All climates in revolving years
Know not themselves; Nations change their faces;
But the Earth is safe, and preserves its All;
Neither increased by time, nor worn by Age:
Its motion is not instantaneous,
It fatigues not its Course. – Always the same
It has been, and shall be. – Our father's saw
No alteration, neither shall posterity:
'Tis God, who for ever is immutable."

PRESIDENT.
"PHILOSOPHY, thou Guide of Life! Thou search out
of virtue! Thou expeller of vice! What, not only
would become of us, but even, what would be the
Life of Humanity without thee? Thou has founded
cities; thou has gathered disperses mankind into a

Society of Life. Thou has united them to each other, first by a participation of the same abode, afterward by wedlock, and finally, by a communion of letters and words. Thou has been the Giver of Laws, and the Mistress of Manners and Discipline. We have recourse to thee, we implore thy Aid, we devote ourselves entirely to thee. One day spent well, and according to thy dictates, is to be preferred to a prevaricating[97] immortality. Whose riches should we rather use than thine? Thou, I say, that has granted us a *perfect Tranquility of Life*, and has exempted us from the *Terrors of Death*."

RESPONDENT.
REASON is the true and first Law,
The Light and Splendor of Life.

PRESIDENT.
"Think not, (as you often seen recounted in Fables) that those who have been guilty of wicked actions, are scared and agitated by the flaming Torches of Furies. Every man's own fraud, every man's own terror, disturbs him most; every man's own wickedness spurs him on to madness; his own bad thoughts, and the conscience of the mind fill him with dismal apprehensions. These are the constant and domestics *Furies* of the Wicked,"

---

97 *Prevaricating* – a deliberate "bend" of truth; falsehood. Also note, the statement in text (possibly quoting *Cicero*) compares to the "Thousands" verses from the Buddhist *Dhammapada*, for example: It is better to live one day as free person, than one-thousand days as a slave. It is better to live one day in Truth, than one-thousand living in falsehood, &tc.

RESPONDENT.
To lead a happy Life, virtue alone is sufficient,
And is to itself an ample reward.

PRESIDENT.
What is honest is the sole good.

RESPONDENT.
Neither is there any Thing useful but what is
laudable.

PRESIDENT.
Now, (dearly beloved *Brethren*) the Philosophical
Canon is to be distinctly read, it must be weighed
attentively, and must stand the test of your
judgment.

RESPONDENT.
As the contemplation of the nature of Things is
agreeable, so also it is a most useful science: By
attention, therefore, we shall weigh and judge.

PRESIDENT.
"The ancient Philosophers, in order to discuss what
NATURE was, divided it into two Things: The one
efficient, the other that which is *effected*. To that
which effects they supposed a *Force*[98] inherent, and
to that which is effected, a certain *Matter*; to both

---

98 "*Force* is in reality *Motion*; for as there's no Force without
Motion, so the whole Force of Matter exerts itself by Motion.
Body is taken sometimes in a broad sense for *Matter*; but it
signifies for the most part a certain Portion of Matter, made up
of many simple substances, so that Matter and Body are very
often confused." (From the original notes to the 1751 edition.)

notwithstanding both inherent; for *Matter* itself cannot cohere, unless contained by some *Force*, nor *Force* without some *Matter*, as every Thing is compelled to be somewhere, the result of both they call a *Body*, and as it were a certain *quality*."

"Some of these *qualities* are original, other *derived from them*. The original are of one king and simple: The derived from them are various, and of manifold shapes. *Air, Fire, Water* and *Earth* are therefore original, and from them spring the *Forms of Animals*, and all those Things that are generated from the Earth, wherefore they are called *Beginnings* and *Elements*, of which *Air* and *Fire* have the Force of *moving* and *effecting* the other Parts, that of *receiving*, and as it were, of being *passive*, I mean the *Water* and *Earth*."[99]

"But they imagine a certain *Matter without any species, and devoid of all that quality* to be comprised in all,[100] out of which all Things are extracted, and by which all Things are effected, capable of *receiving* all, and imparting to them all kinds of *changes*,

---

99 "The *Air, Fire, Water* and *Earth*, are improperly taken for Elements, as we have shown in the *preliminary dissertation*. The *Water* and *Earth* are not said to be passive, as if absolutely ever at rest; but because Motion in them affects not alike the senses, as in *Fire* and *Air*." (From the original notes to the 1751 edition.)

100 "*The First Matter* consists in all the indivisible particles of every species, by whose conjunction and disjunction, all mixed bodies are made, these without ceasing are resolved into one another, saving though always the constituent parts, which neither can be divided nor annihilated." (From the original notes to the 1751 edition.)

undergoing also the same *dissolution*, not *annihilation*, but rather a *reproduction* of Things into their own parts, which can be cut and divided *in infinitum*, inasmuch as the minutest Thing in Nature can suffer a division."

"What's moved, moves in *spaces*, which can be divided also *in infinitum*,[101] and as that *Force*, which we called *quality*, is so moved and agitated up and down, backwards and forwards, so must likewise all and every part of *Matter*, and thus conjointly effect the Things that are called *qualia*: Out of which, in every *coherent* and *continued* nature, with all its parts, the *World* was made; externally to which there's no part of *matter*, nor no *body* existing."

"All the Things that are in the World are *Parts* of the World,[102] and comprised in an *intelligent* nature, endowed with perfect *Reason*, and the same *Eternal*; for there's nothing strong to bring it to destruction: This Force they call the *Soul* of the *World*, as also a *Mind*, and perfect *Wisdom*, and consequently God."

---

101 "The *spaces* of *determinations*, or *boundaries*, (though all Things are in a perpetual motion, not one point in the Universe being absolutely at rest) are the cause that no species of motion is infinite, although all motions taken together can be properly denominates as *infinite Action*." (From the original notes to the 1751 edition.)

102 "The Parts of the Universe are either integrant, or constituent, no void being placed between them, from whose motions and affections a truly divine harmony arises, which cannot be dissolved by any stronger cause, as none such exists out of the infinite Whole." (From the original notes to the 1751 edition.)

"To this REASON they attribute, as it were, a certain *prudent knowledge* of all the Things that are subject to it,[103] and therefore suppose, that first and principally it takes care of celestial Things, and afterward on Earth of what belongs to humans: This *administration* is sometimes called by them, Necessity, because nothing can happen contrary to what it has appointed, *as being a fatal and immutable continuation of the everlasting Order.* Sometimes it is termed Fortune, because it executes many Things unexpectedly with regard to us, upon account of the obscurity and our ignorance of true Causes."

RESPONDENT.
The nature of the *efficient*, no more than that of the *effect*, leaves us hereafter no room for doubt.

PRESIDENT.
We must set forth the praises of the heavenly Origin of *Souls*, infused into the greatest and the smallest.

PRES. & RESP.
Some thing by these appearances induced,
That to the Bees an energy divine,
And part of the Celestial Mind, is given;
For that a God, diffused through all the Mass,
Pervades the Earth, the Sea, and Deep of Air:
Hence humans, and cattle, herds, and savage beasts,

---

103 "The Force and Energy of the Whole sometimes receives the name of *providence*, which so disposes celestial and terrestrial Things, that are administered with the greatest Reason, and no room left for either chance or fortune, every Thing acting by a liberty free from co-action." (From the original notes to the 1751 edition.)

All at their births receive Ethereal Life;
Hither again, dissolved, they back return;
Nor Death takes place; but, all immortal, fly
To Heaven, and in their proper Stars reside.

PRESIDENT.
Let us now make honorable mention of those men
and women among the ancients, who taught or
acted nobly.[104]

RESPONDENT.
That they may benefit us by their example, as well
as learning.

PRESIDENT.
The sacred memory of *N.*[105]

---

104 The material immortality observed in Mystery Traditions
since the most ancient of current civilizations in Mesopotamia
and Egypt was based on "ancestral memory" and we can see
this evident in many of the other mystical and religious
cultural traditions. The "remembrance" of those demonstrating
higher minds and abilities is what granted their "immortality"
on Earth by passing knowledge and demonstrations down to
further generations. In such, their memory remains forever and
is ingrained in the "evolution" of the human species, or rather
the continuation of the "sacred knowledge" maintained in the
"Ancient Mystery Schools" that it should not be lost to politics
and religion of the surface world (Realm).

105 This tradition of remembrance is often performed culturally
and and ancestrally or specific to one's own tradition. In
Roman Catholicism, the same practice is observed to honor the
immortality of those they have deemed *saints*. In the current
example, Toland is passing to us a tradition marked by the
classical philosophers, and so the names evoked are *Greek* and
Roman – Socrates, Plato, Xenophon, Caro, Cicero... Selmo,
Thales, Anaximander, Xenophanes, Melissus, Ocellus,
Democritus, Parmenides, Dicaerchus, Confucius, Cleobulina,

RESPONDENT.
May it tend to our advantage.

PRESIDENT.
Let us praise all other philosophical companies, and
commemorate the male and female Votaries of
Truth.

RESPONDENT.
Let the praiseworthy be praised and honored.

PRESIDENT.
Let us toast the Muses.

RESPONDENT.
Come, we'll drink it moderately.

Theano, Pamphila, Cerellia, Hypatia... (The call to the name
and the response is repeated for each name.)

MARDUKITE

– III –

THE THIRD PART OF THE FORM
(OF CELEBRATING THE SOCRATIC-SOCIETY)

THE LIBERTY OF THE SOCIETY;
and
A LAW, NEITHER DECEIVING,
NOR TO BE DECEIVED

PRESIDENT.
We must always wish,
That there should be a *sound Mind*,
in a *sound Body*.
And as *Life* is not to be laid down on a slight pretext,
So *Death* is never to be dreaded.

RESPONDENT.
Nothing more is to be wished for.
And to effect this, we must use our utmost
endeavors.

PRESIDENT.
Let us therefore sing joyfully and tuneably.

PRES. & RESP.
The man in conscious virtue bold,
Who dares his secret purpose hold,
Unshaken heard the crowd's tumultuous cries,
And the impetuous tyrant's angry brow defies.

Let the loud winds, that rule the seas,
Their wild tempestuous horrors raise;
Let Jove's[106] dread arm with Thunder
rend the Spheres,
Beneath the crush of worlds, undaunted he appears.

PRESIDENT.
Among the wise,
Mirth is more esteemed than Gain.

RESPONDENT.
Mirth is the characteristic of a free man,
Sadness that of a slave.

PRESIDENT.
'Tis better to *ruler over* none,
than to be any man's *slave*.

RESPONDENT.
One may live honorably without a *servant*;
But there is no living at any rate with a *master*.

PRESIDENT.
But 'tis necessary to obey the laws,
For without them, there's no property, no safety.[107]

---

106 *Jove* – "Jupiter" or "Zeus" in the Olympian Pantheon; also
"Enlil" or specifically "Marduk" in the Babylonian (Anunnaki)
Pantheon of Mesopotamia; elsewhere as Thor for the Norse
Germans, &tc. As the largest *Celestial Body* in the local solar
system, the Celestial Pantheon was fashioned to mark its
heights with it. Knowing that its movements control the
greatest gravitational force on local *Celestial Spheres* it is
deemed the "leader" of the group.

107 Although considered *tyrannical* at first glance, the revolution
installation of early law and justice, made famous in the

RESPONDENT.
We are therefore *servants* of the Laws,
That we may be *free*.

PRESIDENT.
There is as wide a different between
liberty as *licentiousness*.[108]

RESPONDENT.
As between *liberty* and *slavery*.

PRESIDENT.
Hear, therefore, (noble equals) consider with
yourselves, and always show in your actions, the
unerring rule for living well, dying happily, and
doing all Things properly. A Rule, I say, not to be
deceived, and Law never deceiving, to be delivered
to you now, in the very words, in which formerly
Marcus Tullius inimitably expressed it.

RESPONDENT.
With open ears, and hearts erect, we shall listen.

PRESIDENT.
"Right Reason is the only *true Law*, a Law befitting
Nature, extended to all, consistent with itself, and
everlasting. A Law that invites men to their duty by

---

ancient world as the "*Code of Hammurabi*" was not intended
to suppress the populations, but to protect them. New for its
time, the *Code of Law* established rights for people and their
property in the realm ('real estate') in addition to the rights of
wives and other civic institutions that we now take for granted
in the modern world.

108 *Licentiousness* – blatantly immoral behavior and lawless
unrestraint.

commanding, and deters from fraud by forbidding. A Law that commands or forbids not in vain the honest, and on the contrary, by commanding or forbidding moves not the dishonest."

"It is not lawful to obrogate[109] this Law, nor derogate any thing from it, nor wholly abrogate it. Neither can we, by the senate or people, be exempted from the Law."

"We are not to seek for any other explainer, or interpreter of this Law, but itself; it is not a different Law at *Rome*, from what it is at *Athens*, nor different now, from what it shall be hereafter: But one and the same Law, eternal and immortal, has and shall contain all times and nations."

"There shall be one, as it were, common *Master* and *Ruler of All*, that *God*, the inventor, umpire, and *Giver* of this *Law*: He who obeys not this Law is his own enemy, he scorns the nature of man, and therefore shall undergo the greatest punishments, though he escapes all other supposed ones."

RESPONDENT.
We are willing to be brought up,
and governed by this Law, not by the lying, and
superstitious fictions of men.

---

109 *Obrogate* – "The sense of *Obrogo.*" To modify or change a law by proposing the "Enacting of a Law" in contrary to the former.

PRESIDENT.
Laws framed by men, are neither clear,
nor universal; Nor always the same,
nor ever efficacious.[110]

RESPONDENT.
They are therefore useful to few, or wholly to none.
Interpreters alone, excepted.

PRESIDENT.
Be still attentive. "Superstition," says *Tully*, (whose
words are unquestionably true) "overspreading
nations, seized upon almost the minds of all, and
took possession of the weakness of men. This is
evident from my Books upon the *Nature of the Gods*,
and I have cleared it up to my utmost in this
dissertation: For I flattered myself, that I should
conduce not a little to my own particular advantage,
and that of my country, if I could find a means to
root it out entirely. Not that it should be
understood, that by destroying superstition, religion
is also destroyed, for it is a wise man's business to
uphold the institutions of his ancestors, and retain
their rites and ceremonies; but what I intimate is,
that the beauty of the world, and Order of heavenly
Things, force us to confess, that there exists an
excellent and *Eternal Nature*, which should be the
object of the contemplation and admiration of all
mankind. Wherefore, as the *religion* is to be
propagated, that's joined to the Knowledge of
Nature, so all the roots of *superstition* are to be
plucked out, and cast away."

---

110 *Efficacious* – having or showing the desired result, or
otherwise *effective*.

RESPONDENT.
The superstitious man, asleep or awake,
enjoys no repose:
He lives not happily, Nor dies securely,
Who, living and dying, is a prey to silly priests.

PRESIDENT.
Whatever time, Nature has allotted every Man for
Life, –

RESPONDENT.
– He should be satisfied with it.

PRESIDENT.
He who dreads what cannot be avoided, can never
possess a sedate mind.[111]

RESPONDENT.
But he who fears not Death, because necessary,
prepares a safeguard for a happy Life.

PRESIDENT.
As our birth brought us the Beginning of all things,
so shall our Death the End.[112]

RESPONDENT.
As nothing of these belonged to us before our birth,
so nothing shall after Death.

---

111 As in the Welsh Triad of the Bardic Druids; The three things
avoided by the wise: fearing the inevitable, expecting the
impossible, and grieving the irretrievable.

112 The messages are thematic to close the *Form*, and speak in
terms of civic law now, nothing philosophically – since
nothing truly dies.

PRESIDENT.
He is a great fool who weeps;
He shall not be a live a thousand years hence.

RESPONDENT.
As he who weeps,
That he has not lived to a thousand years.

PRESIDENT.
To fame, and custom only, funeral pomps and
solemnities should be granted, –

RESPONDENT.
– They are therefore to be despised by us; But not to
be neglected.

PRESIDENT.
Let us toast some Health.

RESPONDENT.
Come.

PRESIDENT.
My humble Service to the SOCIETY.

- - - - - - -

RESPONDENT.
It shall go round in full bumpers.[113]

---

113 Notes toward the revolving presidency of the Society (if
applicable).

PRESIDENT.
Let the new President give orders for all other particulars.

REPONDENT.
It shall be done.[114]

---

114 "Afterwards they feast temperately, *teaching one another and learning*, which is the symbol and principle Scope of the Society." (From the original notes to the 1751 edition.)

EPILOGUE – SUPPLEMENTAL KNOWLEDGE

OF A TWO-FOLD PHILOSOPHY OF THE PANTHEISTS
(THAT IS TO BE FOLLOWED)

I.

We have, in the *preliminary dissertation*,[115] with as much conciseness, as perspicuity, discussed the nature, regulation, and names of private *Societies*, or learned Entertainments among the *Greeks* and *Romans*; and, at the same time, we have not concealed the state or origin of the modern *Socratic Society*, which we made the chief subject of our discourse. By the extraordinary *Form* of this society, now first brought to light, any one may see plainly that the manners of the *Brethren* are not morose, rather, polite and elegant, nay even devoid of all vice and just censure.

Moreover the law of this agreeable banquet, not less just than prudent, are to be learned; and the attractive charms of liberty, far remote from all licentiousness, are to be thoroughly read, so much the more, as nothing is so prized by the *Brotherhood*, as not only the cultivating of modesty, continence, justice, and all kinds of virtues themselves, but also of exciting others, as well by words as example, to their practice. But they treat of all these human Things humanely.

You shall have jokes without gall,

---

115 Given within the current edition as the "*Prologue – Preliminary Knowledge.*"

and liberty not to be dreaded in the morning,
and no restraint laid upon your tongue.

You may perceive, that their "religion" is simple, clear, easy, without blemish, and freely bestowed, not painted over, not intricate, embarrassed, incomprehensible, or mercenary; not luring minds with silly fables, and ensnaring them by the filth, inhumanity, or ridicule of superstition; not subservient, I say, to the private advantage of any family, or faction, against the public good; not scandalizing or railing at, much less disturbing or tormenting any person or persons, so that they be honest and peaceable men. There is no occasion to make a longer discourse upon the Improvement of the Mind.

The PANTHEISTS can deservedly be styled the *Mysts* and *Hierophants* of Nature;[116] for as formerly the *Druids*, men o fan elevated genius, kept up to the strictness of their brotherly union, (as the authority of *Pythagoras* has decreed) so also they were versed in the knowledge of the most abstruse Things, and their Minds were lifted up by the contemplation of the sublimest mysteries. The *Socratic* companions strenuously ruminate upon the same studies, for which the *Druids* and *Pythagorics* made themselves so illustrious, both instituted Societies, yet the *Pantheists* allow not all their words and deeds; for where they depart from Truth, there we also depart from them, praising voluntarily what we approve of, and

---

116 *Priests* – "Those that are learned themselves, or instruct others in the mysteries (of religion); an interpreter of the sacred mysteries." (From the original notes to the 1751 edition.)

giving thanks to those, by whose labor we have in any shape benefited ourselves.

II.

But perhaps it may be imputed as a fault to the PAN-THEISTS for embracing two doctrines, the one *External* or popular,[117] adjusted in some measure to the prejudices of the people, or to Doctrines publicly authorized for true; the other *Internal* or philosophical,[118] altogether conformable to the nature of Things, and therefore to Truth itself: And moreover for proposing this secret philosophy, naked and entire, unmasked, and without any tedious circumstance of words, in the recesses of a private chamber, to men only of consummate probity and prudence. But what person, unless equally ignorant of the disposition of the human genius, and what's transacted in Nature, doubts that they act wisely? The reason of what I say is manifest. For no religion, no sect, can brook a contradiction, much less can endure that their doctrines should be charged with error or falsity, and their ceremonies with vanity or folly.

All Things are send down to them from Heaven, although they gape after earthly desires. They are divine (if you credit them) and indispensably necessary for the regulation of Life, although it is evident that they are human, empty also, and superfluous, and often monstrous fictions: nay even, for the most

---

117 *External* – "Exoterica."
118 *Internal* – "Esoterica."

part, destructive to the common and public tranquility, as it appears to a demonstration from daily
experience. Among so many various and disagreeing
opinions, if it is possible that none of them should be
true, at least it is impossible that more than one of
them should be true: This is an acute observation
long ago made by *Tully*, in discussing the Nature of
the Gods.

Wherefore the PANTHEISTS, persons of the strictest
moderation, behave towards frantic, foolish, and
stubborn men, as fond nurses do towards their bab-
bling minions, who imbibe from them the pleasing
infatuation of imagining themselves kings and
queens, that they are the only Papa and Mama's
Pets, and that there are none so pretty and so fine as
they. Those who do not flatter infants in these trifles
are odious and disagreeable to them. Those, on the
other hand, who do adhere not by line and level[119] to
the opinions of the ignorant, although adults, are
abominated and ill used; their inveteracy[120] is
brought to such a pitch, that they deign not to keep
them company, they oblige them with no office of
humanity, they would fain have them, while alive,
prohibited Fire and Water, and, when dead, etern-
ally tormented.[121]

---

119 *Line and Level* – Meaning "exactly as given," or the precise
specifications prescribed by others; also "a-for-a" or "one-to-
one."

120 *Inveteracy* – "Habitual, hardened, established, rooted, fixed;
or set in place."

121 *Tormented* – Or "banished" from memory after dead (once
first given no position of esteem in life).

But as *superstition* is always the same in vigor,[122] though sometimes different in rigor,[123] and as no wise man's attempt was amiss in rooting it out of the minds of all persons, which could not be compassed at any rate; yet he'll use his endeavors to do all that can be done, that is, by plucking out the teeth and paring the nails of his worst and most pernicious of monsters, he will not suffer it at its pleasure to hurt on every side.

It is to men in power, and politicians actuated with this noble Disposition of Mind, that we are indebted for all the *religious liberty*, that is any where now a days to be met with, which has redounded[124] not a little to the great advancement of letters, commerce, and civil concord. Whereas, on the contrary, to the superstitious, or pretended worshipers of supreme powers, I mean, to spirit-haunted enthusiasts, or scrupulously pious, are owing all feuds, animosities, mutinies, mulcts,[125] rapines,[126] stigmates,[127] imprisonments, banishments, and deaths.

---

122 *Vigor* – "Strength, force, active energy, vitality."

123 *Rigor* – "Severity, strictness, harshness, rigidity."

124 *Redounded* – "Consequential results or affects, such as those (good or bad) from a person's actions," or later the results of the words and deeds that are affecting long after (the original instance).

125 *Mulct* – "Fines and penalties; usually such as collected by fraud or extortion

126 *Rapines* – "Plunder, Pillage; essentially the violent seizure of someone else's property."

127 *Stigmates, stigma* – "A stain on someone's reputation; alternatively in ancient times, a brand put on criminals."

Thus it necessarily must happen, *That one Thing should be in the Heart, and in a private meeting; and another Thing abroad, and in public assemblies.* This maxim has often been greatly in vogue, and practiced not by the ancients alone; for to declare the Truth, it is more in use among the moderns, although they profess it is less allowed.

III.

Having thus briefly established the two-fold philosophy of the ancients, it will be no difficult matter to understand, that the PANTHEISTS, among so many different sects in vogue, and their mutual scuffles, I wish not massacres and carnage, lead a peaceable life, and neither hurried away by a love for those, not a hatred for these, study the safety of the Republic, and the common good of mankind, sword enemies of all debates and parties.

If those who are going astray, are pleased to be put upon the right road, they will courteously point it out to them; if they persist in their error, they will, notwithstanding, friendly and from their hearts exercise a commerce of life with them.[128] They know,

---

128 The human mind is incapable of seeing past the point it doesn't understand, or rather (and worse) misunderstand. As such, the experience of reality, and its understanding by that mind, is collapsed, interpreted or reduced to the individual's own ability to understand and understanding properly (a-for-a, one-to-one, with what is actually taking place). As such, those refusing and incapable of seeing things at a "higher, wide-angle, more encompassing" scale, as it applies to the nature of existence, it is virtually impossible to impose this on them. We

and lay it down for a principle, that no man is to be disdained or scorned upon account of indifferent and harmless opinions, and that whatever nation or religion he is of, his company, for the virtues and excellence of his mind, is to be sought after, and in no wise to be avoided, but for his vices, and the corruption of his morals.[129] Therefore a *Pantheist* will never punish or disgrace any man for a mere sentiment; for sayings, I say, or actions that hurt no man, neither will he advise or instigate others to defile themselves by such a notorious piece of villainy.

Fraudulent priests, or impotent silly women, may stir up magistrates against them, not able to the same time to lay any crime to their charge, or upbraid[130] them with any thing, except that they cannot solve their objections, or because they live a life more agreeable to the dictates of reason, and more uprightly than they themselves do. But none

---

can accept and love them and respect a right to life, of course, but philosophically, there is no point in involving them in higher work. Their own ignorance is markedly a personal yield to "equality" of all opinions, which on an esoteric level (within this book) has already been shown to be implausible. Notice how the civic notion of all-encompassing "equality" is never called for by the higher echelons of a Society, only for the lower who believe (even if intuitively) that they are "missing out" on something. Hence we now have a two-way street displaying both a need for "private work" by the learned, while equally being guessed at by the "conspiracy theories" of the uninitiated public.

129 Let men think what they will, judging with rewards and punishments subject only to their *behavioral deviation* (either "above" or "below") from the civic societal standards set forth (usually by a specific culture or nature).

130 *Upbraid* – "To severely reproach; to blame or lay fault with."

in a public employ, or charged with the interest of the public, will give ear to these brain-sick fantastic persons, unless he is a man blinded by superstition, or, on the other hand, a slave to ambition and filthy gain, and consequently regardless of the honor that is due to virtue and merit.[131]

As for the rest, the *Socratic Companions* laying no stress upon the praise and scandal of others, make it their total endeavor to live after their own, and not another's fancy, continued with their lot: They correct their hearts with virtuous precepts, and embellish their minds with learning, the better, and with greater ease, to be serviceable to themselves, their friends, and all persons; to approach, moreover, (though they should never attain to it) with more certainty, and nearer to that perfection, which every good and learned man is obliged to have at heart, and wish for, either to acquire it for himself, or to impart it to others.

Cicero, to whom our *Society* is indebted to for so many, and such excellent things, towards the end of his *First Book of Laws*, has furnished us with *A distinct, and exact idea of the best and most accomplished man.* Let the Learned then read, and form themselves according to this Rule.

---

131 Opinions are all fine and good until action is employed and then consequently there is very much a "right" and "wrong" way about things.

IV.

"He who knows himself,[132] will first suppose that he has something Divine, and he will think in himself, that his genius is consecrated like any image of worship; and he will always act and think in a manner worthy of so great a favor of the gods."

"And when he has thoroughly known, and wholly proved himself,[133] he will understand how Nature has set him off for life, and what considerable means he has to obtain and acquire *wisdom*, inasmuch as, at first, he imbibed in his Mind, an imperfect knowledge of all Things,[134] adorned by which, and guided by *Wisdom*, let him show himself, according as his soul makes a greater progress towards perfection, a better man, and, as a necessary consequence of his goodness, let him contemplate his happiness."

"For when his Mind, formed by knowledge and price of virtue, has quitted its fondness and indulgence for the body, has laid a restraint upon please, as a stain to beauty, has made void the terrors of death and pain, has entered into a *Society of Love* with its own, has reputed all its own, whom Nature has united by a mutual benevolence, has embraced the true worship of the deity, and the purity of religion, and has sharpened the edge of wit as well as the eyes, to choose good and reject the contrary, (which virtue,

---

132 Self-awareness. Knowing "I am."

133 Has proved to himself "the faculties of the mind." (Quoting original notes to the 1751 edition.)

134 "Ideas and notions." (From the original notes to the 1751 edition.)

from its forecast, is called *prudence*) – What situation can be said or thought to possess a more extensive happiness?"

"The same accomplished man, when with due consideration he has taken a view of the heavens, earth, seas, the nature of all things, the causes of their generation, where they run back again, when, and how, they are to be dissolved, what is mortal and perishable in them, what divine and heavenly: When he has almost laid hold of the *Being* that rules and governs these Things, when he has discovered himself to be not inclosed within one wall, the native of any circumscribed place, but a citizen of the whole World, as one city: In this magnificent appearance of Things; and in this contemplation and knowledge of Nature, ye immortal powers! How well he shall know himself![135] How he shall despise, scorn, and repute as nothing, what commonly is deemed the height of pomp and grandeur!"

"As by a kind of ramp,[136] he'll fortify all these particulars with staunch arguments, a just discernment of truth and falsehood, and a certain science and art of understanding: He'll know what conclusions he is to draw from his premises, and what is repugnant to every Thing."

"As he's sensible, that he is born for civil society, he will not only enter into the discussion of these mat-

---

135 "An advice imparted to us by the *Pythean,* Apollo." (From the original notes to the 1751 edition.)

136 *Ramp* – ("*rampire*") meaning a "ladder of knowledge" or "logic."

ters, by the subtleties of dispute, but also by a continued discourse, bu which he may rule people,
establish laws, chastise the wicked, defend the good,
praise illustrious men, deliver wholesome precepts
and persuasive encomiums[137] to his citizens, exhort
to honor, recall from wickedness, comfort the afflic-
ted, and exhibit, by everlasting monuments, the
transactions and ordinances of the brave and wise,
to the indelible disgrace of the wicked."

"Now as so many and such mighty Things are per-
ceivable in man, by those who are willing to know
themselves, we must necessarily conclude, that *Wisdom* is both their parent, and the nurse that trains
them up."

V.

But who is it, that would not be willing to be more
wise and better? Who is it that could not? And
where's the end of any discipline, but to make men
wise and good? If it is deficient in these respects, it
seems to me for the greater part useless, though not
entirely for ornament and elegance sake to be rejected.

Wherefore the PANTHEIST become wise, or at least
possessed of the next degree to Wisdom, shall not, in
the first place, to his prejudice, run counter to the
received *Theology*, that in philosophical matters
swerves from Truth; neither shall be altogether be

---

137 *Encomium* – "formal expressions of high praise; such as in a
    eulogy."

silent, when a proper occasion presents itself; yet he shall never run the risque[138] of his life, but in defense of his country and friends.

As to the Most Holy Maxims, which are ever and always to be professed, without addition, we will not speak openly of them here. Secondly, all the Truths that the *Pantheist* <u>can</u> with safety disclose, as politics, astronomy, mechanics, economics, and such like, he shall not only not envy them to others, but even voluntarily communicate them, still never without a due caution, because the commonality weighs most Things in the scales of opinion,[139] and but very few in those of Truth. Finally, he shall exactly estimate, and in the silence of his heart, meditate upon the most sacred dogmas, regarding either the nature of *God*, or of the *Soul*; and he shall not make the wicked, nor the ignorant, not any, except the *Brethren* alone, or other ingenious, upright, and learned men, *Partakers of Esoterics*.

I am conscious to myself, that this silence, and prudent reservedness of Mind, will not be agreeable to all persons; however the PANTHEISTS shall not be more open, until they are at full liberty to think as they please, and speak as they think.

---

138 Probably "risk."

139 Care must be taken in demonstrating executions, actions and innovations in the surface world (Realm) because the Truth is rarely of "common opinion" which is what is given reign in the world of the masses, albeit falsely.

VI.

Perhaps, one more curious, than considerate, should ask, whether in effect such a society exists? Whether the *Form* we exhibited is there recited?

To clear up the matter in brief: there are, undoubtedly, in several places, not a few *Pantheists*, who, according to the custom of others, have their private assemblies and societies, where they feast together, and what is the sweetest kind of sauce, where they philosophic over it. Whether or not that *Form* or any *Part* of it is always, and every where recited among them, I leave undecided. But, for your part, reader, whoever you are, make use of it, and I heartily wish, that it may tend to your advantage...

APPENDIX

SELECTIONS FROM THE CLIDOPHORUS

OF THE EXOTERIC AND ESOTERIC PHILOSOPHY
(EXTERNAL AND INTERNAL DOCTRINES
OF THE ANCIENTS)

I.

To know the Truth is one thing, to tell it others is another thing: and as all men profess to admire the first, so few men practice the last as they ought. At the same time the Truth is owned to be more valuable than wealth or honor, there are by most without hesitation preferred before it, which appears not only by their eager application to procure riches and titles, while they abandon the study of Truth, or faintly pursue it: but also by the abject deference they shamelessly pay to men of power, and the indifference or neglect they commonly show to men of learning.

For men being observed to be naturally fond of Truth, through laziness or other occupations, few are capable to acquire the possession of it; some cunning persons thought they could not better attain to authority over the rest (which draws riches after it of course) than by pretending to be masters of this same Truth. Next, they dispersed what they could impart to others, without putting them to any labor, or diverting them from any business: and as for a little expense, who would grudge to give a

price out of his transitory self for the invaluable
jewel of knowledge? Or not think it equitable to be-
stow a moderate reward on men, that could equally
delight and benefit him? Nor did these crafty empir-
ics stop here.

They knew the falsity of facts, and the fallacy of
reasoning, might at one time or another be detected
by men of penetration. Wherefore, as the Devil is
God's ape, they boasted of a superior and supernatural knowledge, not subject to the rules of criticism,
nor a proper object of understanding. Nay, they
went to a greater length, openly maintaining that it
was lawful to lie for the public good, to that the
common people being incapable of reflection, out to
be managed by guile, and to be deluded by agreeable
fables into obedience to their governors.

Thus *Mnevis*, an Egyptian king, imposed on his subjects, by feigning an extraordinary communication
with heaven. *Zoroaster* successfully practiced the
same art. *Pythagoras*, after hiding himself for some
time (as if he were dead) appeared again at Crotona,
preaching the joys and torments of another life. His
disciple *Zamolxis* vaunted having received divine
revelations in a cave, whereby he gained such authority, as to prescribe what laws he pleased to the
Scythians. *Minos* and *Epimenides* in Crete, published
the conferences they had with *Jupiter* in their several
retirements from the society of other men, on whom
they obtruded their own fictions for divine commands. [A very long list of examples could be
appended here, including the manner of which it
may have been passed down from the *Mesopotamians*

and *Egyptians* unto the *Greeks* then *Romans* and so forth. Even *Moses* can be, at least on the surface, listed among these examples.]

The Priests, for their own interest, were not wanting any where to promote such penal laws; and the magistrates (partly through superstition proceeding from their ignorance; and partly through policy, to grasp at more power than the laws allowed, by the assistance of the Priests) have been commonly and ready to enforce those laws, by what they called *wholesome severities.* Hence no room was left for the propagating of Truth, except at the expense of a man's life, or at least of his honor and employments, whereof numerous examples may be alleged.

The Philosophers therefore, and other well-wishers to mankind in most nations, were constrained by this holy tyranny to make use of a "two-fold doctrine; the one *popular*, accommodated to the prejudices of the vulgar, and to the received customs or religions: the other *philosophical*, conformable to the nature of things, and consequently to Truth; which, with doors fast shut and under all other precautions, they communicated only to friends of known probity, prudence and capacity."[140]

---

140 A distinction prevalent throughout the *Pantheisticon* texts, "generally called the *Exoteric* and *Esoteric*, or the *External* and *Internal Doctrines*."

II.

Although men may profess the religion of Him who is *Truth* it self, and whose service is perfect *Freedom* – they are commanded to *Love* each other, and to speak the *Truth* one to another: but they obey, as if they were expressly attached to the contrary. Not only does every sect furiously oppose another, but those of the same sect stand in mutual opposition for the poorest trifles in the world, for airy distinctions, for a party-jargon, for favor, and oftentimes for syllables and letters. They manifest all the signs of a perfect hatred, by branding, defaming, and avoiding each other; their leaders ever showing them the example, as if they were afraid they should come to a better understanding, and sooner or later perceive that they quarreled about nothing.

These are facts not possible to be denied. And as little can it be denied, that, not content wit this rancor of mind, or the narrowness of their peculiar schemes and notions; they heartily plague each other with fines and incapacities, with exile, imprisonment, and other numberless ways: not to mention the last of all evils, Death, which at least is so in their opinion; till persecution ends at length in the *Inquisition*, as the utmost perfection of this hellish *economy of faith*.

Daily experience sufficiently shows that there is no declaring of Truth in most places, but at the hazard of a man's reputation, employment or life. These circumstances cannot fail to beget the woeful effects of insincerity, dissimulation, gross ignorance, and licentious barbarity. What's most of all to be lamented, is, that but too much of this ferments in the purest *churches.*

Among *Priests* and *ministers* in particular (leaving every one to assume the name he likes best, for they are no more agreed about names than any thing else) what unmanly pumping and tale-bearing, what wire-drawing to an acknowledgment of their thoughts, and deposing them if they are frank, or suspecting them if reserved? Of necessity this produces shifting, ambiguities, equivocations, and hypocrisy in all its shapes; which will not merely be called, but actually esteemed, *necessary cautions*: occasioned in all times and places by ambitious *Priests,* supported by their property the mob; thus depriving us of the peace of life and the truth of religion, and of philosophical discoveries and improvement, to the no small detriment of mankind.

"There is more stress to be laid on any miracles received and approved by the Church (as the cure of a slight ague[141] *divinely wrought) than if any man should see all who died in this age brought to life again, than if mountains were removed out of their places; than if a new world was created: since in all these things there would still remain the suspicion of magical fraud, whence they might be deemed not really performed (which one would think were earlier suspected of an ague) but rather to be the fancies of our imaginations, or the illusions of our senses."*[142]

---

141 *Ague* – "a fitful illness or fever; such as may produce hallucinations."

142 Quoting *Berigardus*, in his *"Circulus Pisanus."* Toland

III.

Wherefore *Parmenides* was unquestionably in the right, when he affirmed that *there are two sorts of Philosophy, the one according to Truth, the other according to Opinion*: which is not only true of the *Greeks* and *Romans*, but as certainly so of other nations much more ancient. I know that the words of *Parmenides* may be commodiously understood of the fallaciousness and uncertainty of the senses, which often represent things otherwise than they are in themselves, and must therefore be examined and corrected by *reason*.

From the senses arises *opinion*, and from reason, *demonstration*: on the former are huddled up the prejudices of the vulgar, following the bare appearance of things; on the latter are founded the axioms of the wise, who consider things as they are in themselves. But this is not the twofold philosophy that makes our subject, nor what the author intended, but the other represented by *Philoponus*.

This writer assures us, that *Parmenides* in his *Exoterics* (or books accommodated to the public taste) says *"fire and water are the beginning or principle of all things,"* as if he had acknowledged the world to have been created: but that in his *Esoterics* (or books com-

---

explains about the work that *Berigardus*, "endeavors even to prove, that the being of *God* cannot be known by reason, but only by faith; and that authority of the books of *Scripture* cannot be proved by history or religion, but be implicitly and devoutly received."

piled according to the Truth)[143] he says "*the Universe is one, infinite, and immutable.*" Here not only the distinction of *Exoterics* and *Esoterics* is literally to be learned, but an example of it likewise alleged; namely, a beginning of things *Exoterically*, but *Esoterically*, the eternity and incorruptibility of the Universe.

The Egyptians, who were among the wisest of mortals,[144] had a twofold doctrine: the one secret, and in that very respect "sacred" and the other popular and consequently vulgar. Who is there, that is ignorant of their sacred letters, hieroglyphics, forms, symbols, enigmas, and fables? Far and near was spread the fame of the Egyptian Philosophy, "*Concealing things under the appearance of fables,*" says *Plutarch,* "*and in speeches that contained obscure indications and arguments of the Truth: which they themselves expressly declare, by placing sphynxes before most of their Temples; thus indicating that their doctrine concerning sacred things, consists in a sort of wisdom which is designedly perplexed, and lying hidden under studied veils.*"

That we may give a specimen of such things as they concealed, the *fane of Minerva,* (says Plutarch again) whom they think to be the same with *Isis,* has this

---

143 *Esoterics* – Books and materials written for the learned, not for an appeal to public opinion.

144 *Egyptians* were among the wisest of mortals, also cousin to the *Mesopotamians,* the people called *Sumerians* and in their heights, *Babylonians* and *Chaldeans* – regardless of names, the greatest and most ancient being those that existed prior to the "Classical Era" of the *Greeks* and *Romans.*

inscription that says: "*I am all that was, is, and shall be: Nor has any mortal discovered what is beneath my veil.*" – *Isis* therefore, whom the vulgar believed to have been a "Queen," and of whom they had a thousand different fables; was the *Nature of All Things*, according to the Philosophers, who held the *Universe* to be the principal *God*, or the supreme being, and abstruse or obscure, none seeing beyond the surface of Nature. But this they only discovered to the initiated.

IV.

This double manner of teaching was also in use among other oriental[145] nations, especially the *Ethiopians* and *Babylonians*, the ancient and modern *Brahmins*, the *Syrians*, *Persians*, and the rest, especially those instructed by *Zoroaster*. The classic books, and late travels to this purpose, are in every body's hands. The *Druids* of the *Gauls* and *Britons* would by no means deliver their mysteries or secret doctrines, to any expect the initiated: to say nothing of the *Etruscans*, and other occidental nations, no more than of the present *Chinese*, *Siamese*, and *Indians* properly so called; the thing being so notorious, as to be denied by nobody.

Most celebrated among *Greek* philosophers is the "secret discipline" of *Pythagoras*, after which the original *Aristotelian* "Acroatics," or if you prefer "Acroamatics," have been copied. The disciples of *Py-*

---

145 *Oriental* – in many cases here meaning what is now called the "Ancient Near East."

thagoras were either *Hearers* or *Mathematicians*, or *Exoterical* or *Esoterical*, whom we may render Exterior and Interior auditors. All things were declared to the *Esoterical* (but without witnesses) in a plain, perspicuous, and copious speech: while every thing, on the contrary, was delivered to the *Exoterical*, in a perplexed, obscure, and enigmatic manner; nor was any thing told clearly, except popular and vulgar matters.

"All things ought not to be declared to all men."[146]

They reserved their own doctrines to themselves, as so many holy secrets; or if any other happened to be present, they told their minds to each other by symbols and enigmas or parables: when it has unluckily happened, that scarce any thing which was of use or moment among them, is come to the knowledge of the public; this being the true reason of the obscurity, or rather the almost entire loss of *Pythagorean Philosophy...*

---

146 "The common maxim among them towards all those who were not of their fellowship." (From the original notes to the 1720 edition.)

MARDUKITE

A CRITICAL EXCERPT FROM

NECRONOMICON ANUNNAKI BIBLE
by Joshua Free

THE SECRETS OF THE AGES
&
THE KEY TO IT ALL

I.

Everyone thinks they pretty much have a handle of what's going on in existence. People "believe" they know what they know about any given topic and they base that on their own perceived "experience." They continue to validate things from within that knowledge and things continue to be real within that experience. That's "reality." That's what you perceive to be "real," meaning that your way of perceiving the world will continue to conform to your beliefs about your world, as has been proven time and time again. Energetic currents that exist within all things, whether living or not, this is what you only experience at its most condensed states here in the "physical world" of forms. Therefore, until you remove all filters in self-honesty, you cannot perceive things for what they really are, and semantics and terminology serves as a common stumbling block for the psyche.

This whole question of what is "real" or "not real" is a philosophical problem that affects not only the magickal world and metaphysics but all of science, religion and really any personal perceptions of "truth." In essence, the word "reality" comes from an Indo-European root "reg," (as in "regal," "region," "regular") which is related to a "measuring device" or "ruler" (and also as a "ruler" as in "king"). The word "sane" is related to what is "clean" or "healthy" and functionally it was the purpose of the king or "ruler" of the "real world" or "realm" to set the boundaries of what is "real" and "not real" by which "sanity" might be judged. The conclusion: those who are in agreement or consensus with the realm are healthy and clean and those who are not are mentally ill or insane.

II.

We are told the ancient axiom that: As above; so below. As within; so without. As the Universe; so the self. Know Thyself. Heaven and Hell come from within one's own mind. Life is a mirror – You observe what you reflect. Sciences and technologies shall darken everywhere the hopes of Men. All relationships not in a state of Agreement shall fall. Life experience is subject to belief and belief solidifies, manifests and conditions reality. Self-realization begins with detachment from all things, all systems, all beliefs, all dead memories. You are not your physical body. In a world of depersonalization, You must demonstrate your own self control and determination to regain the freedom of the Self. To be freed from limitations of the world is to make possible the liberation of self in the individual and fusion with the All – One and the same – All-as-One.

III.

Whenever you affirm: "I am..." and add "something" - this is a form of "enslavement to consciousness." The true "I-of-Self" is not restricted to any conception of "persona-personality-programming" that you have "experienced" in the surface reality or world. QED: the true "I of you" has never been "thirsty," never been "angry". Do you want to prove it? The next time you have this "experience," observe it from self. The very idea that you can do this proves it is not "real." If it was from the "I-of-you" it would not be a "thing" to be "observed" by you at all. It would be you! If you can "artificially" create experiences in your mind, what does that tell you?

Self is to be found at the core of your being. It is you who is doing the "discovering" or "finding." It is the self in-and-of self. You are "here in kNow" and when you remove all "things" you find self. It's as simple as that. There is nothing to be "out there" looking for at all. Only when you can see yourself from a point of "self-honesty" can you see you, or anything else for that matter, for what is "real."

IV.

Reality equals Heaven and Earth. Earth is a more physical and seen part of reality. Heaven is more physically unseen. All the dimensions are One. Like one building, and yet there would seem to be vary-ing degrees and levels and doors and barriers and points of perspective indeed. All is one in equality. Reality, space and time is one and whole and we only perceive fragmented parts. The issue is maybe not "what" we are seeing but "why" we are able to see or not see some Thing.

V.

Our emotional responses are reactions based on dead energy, memory and experience. The real is somewhat static or unchanging, yourself is simply "I AM" and there is nothing else but what thought, data and interpretations of the mind based on other people's "experience of the real" provide. This comes to you first by conditioning and then you continue to feed/re-cycle/re-engage yourself in the same knowledge and behavior patterns and build upon them cumulatively.

Your dislikes, likes and inclinations are dictated by the conditioned self, a persona program, recursively operating as a spiral, later to be operantly conditioned (by pleasure = good and pain = bad) until the causal pattern of reality is so deeply ingrained that you become a robot operating on self-fulfilling prophecies and expectation-response triggers. Labels, names and figures are man's calculations of truth. These negate innocence in all forms and are ever-changing.

SYSTEMOLOGY FOR LIFE
by Joshua Free

PATTERNS & CYCLES

I.

Drawing from the observable universe around you, there are two basic concepts that the author is attempting to relay in this NexGen Systemology essay; two semantic instances that are very important in understanding how this new school of philosophy can best assist your life:

> Firstly, the programmed *pattern* of all existence; and secondly, its *cyclic* evolution as observed through time.

Everything that exists does so based on *patterns* operating at various levels or degrees of observation. When observed over *time* by a mind that is calculating and mathematically logical, the magnitude or degree is measured in "intervals" or "phases" that can be compared to one another on *cyclic* terms.

All of existence has the appearance of motion; all things appear to possess attributes of *ebb and flow* as if a tide – but there is a systematic logic behind this appearance, one that is inherent in the very programming of all existence: *a pattern.*

II.

At the most practical level, let us consider for a moment the *behavioral patterns* ingrained or programmed into your personality and how these can be evaluated over time in *cyclic* terms.

Many hundreds – if not thousands – of years of dedicated intellectual work and academia precede us in our pursuits, but underlying all of this 'head knowledge' and 'fancy words' is a desire to not only *predict* human behaviors but actually influence change on the human condition.

These pursuits are most certainly connected; for one reason, they rely on the same data – the same core knowledge base – to be both functional and accurate to any significant probability factor.

When NexGenSys is introduced to the advanced classes,[147] the question of function and purpose is related in the first class on semantics and vocabulary. Often the first questions a student of this new philosophy has when approaching is:

> "How is this going to benefit me in my
> *real world* life?"

They aren't interested in whether or not trees in forests are making sounds; the need for a new philosophy – a new paradigm – was sought, and a new "NexGen" worldview has been wrought.

---

147 Referring to *"Reality Engineering"* by Joshua Free.

III.

Any thinking being can become an *observer* in the ocean of existence – ascertaining knowledge, giving names and making predictions about the validation of those observations and the thought process involved with its interaction. Basically, everyone can determine the readily observable influences that affect them in their lives.

> You wake up in the morning and swing your feet over the edge of your bed making the assumption that there is a solid floor surrounding the plane of slumber on which to plant yourself. If this were not the case, you might find yourself in a bit of trouble – either structurally or existentially!

We make assumptions about our world every day. These are made as a result of the data or knowledge (*pattern*) that we are given by others and then our observation of this data unfold and evolve at the observable scale of the world we call "real" (*cycles*).

The observation of cause and effect in the world is only *true* to the extent that the Observer is capable of understanding. This is not only a matter of intelligence, but there are other requirements for knowledge: a semantic vocabulary in which to communicate experiences accurately and the ability to see the phenomenon in its entirety – holistically – including what is not readily visible 'above the surface'.

IV.

Our personal programming wires in the brain in such a way as to form a "set" or *pattern* by which the experiential world will then be interpreted.

> Two individuals – (a) and (b) – each carrying a unique 'knowledge set' or base, will each understand and communicate an experience (c) in two differing ways – (ac) and (bc).

Neither of which is the true essence of the stimulus – (c) – as it truly is objectively isolated. For it to "exist", *reality* must be *experienced*. The logic for the experience need not be either true or accurate (a for a) to what is *actually* going on in the Universe beneath the surface levels of observable *reality*.

The paradigm encompassing NexGen Systemology is to look *beneath* this very *surface* in question and clearly and self-honestly take in a wide angle, holistic, all inclusive – systematic – way of experiencing the inner world of thought and its relationship with the outer world of forms. As the lens pierces deeper and deeper into the fabric of space and time – *reality* – the continuity, entangled and interconnected nature of these inner and outer realms blurs and we see that the weave and the fabric – the light and the screen – are all, in themselves, composed of the same energetic vibration that spurs out forth from the most primeval and primordial ripple of the void. *Form* came – and the *Pattern* was established.

Humans living in a controlling tyrannical social order are not generally encouraged to question anything about what they are given (told) or to look beneath the surface. We do not truly encourage creativity in our world. It is clearest to communicate in respect to chosen vocabulary – *patterns* and *cycles* – as they apply to our personal psychology and everyday life.

<u>PROBABILITY PATTERNS</u>
Observation of cycles and tendencies to predict a causal relationship or determine the actual condition or flow of dynamic energy using the holistic system as opposed to the understanding of life, reality and existence in isolation or exclusion of perceived parts being separate from other perceived parts.[148]

The fundamental root of all *systemological* applications depends on your ability to determine true and holistic 'probability patterns' that include *all* aspects of a condition – even those outside the 'normative' waking perceptual range available to you with regard to the sensory programs instilled and limitations in physical observation.

> You can only see within your 'range' to see. You can only use what you see to the extent you actually are able to understand information you are receiving.

---

148   Definition from "*Reality Engineering*" by Joshua Free.

V.

Advanced students of NexGen Systemology[149] are taught the concept of *"paradigm parametrics,"* where an experience, phenomenon or condition is being understood in direct relation to a range of possibly experienced *variables* within a model or paradigm. It's similar to describing the unit of measure being used rather than simply offering a numerical value.

> Certainly, 10 centimeters and 10 miles
> are not the same. We must be clear in
> our vision and communications!

In order for Reality to be experienced, it must first be perceived, generally within the parameters, or range of possibility, and processed by some organized method of interpretation, semantics and reasoning, called a paradigm.

> A *paradigm* used to experience or filter
> your reality should be "cleared" to be
> certain you are not thinking "outside"
> of one 'box' only to be trapped in an-
> other...

VI.

CYCLES OF THOUGHT – PATTERNS OF BEHAVIOR

A *paradigm* defines the perspective that is possible of being experienced by the Observer (*Self*). Paradigms

---

149 Referring to *"Reality Engineering"* by Joshua Free.

act as a "baseline" or "set" for all the established 'knowledge' that is accumulated in memory and re-called or retrieved on a continuous basis in order to make sense of the information and energy coming in to form a *reality experience*.

A significant part of your evolution comes from the ability to literally "overcome behaviors," meaning overriding the very programming (*pattern*) of which we are given – either genetically or learned socially. It is this progression of interaction with external en-ergies – our responses and experiences with them – that constitute the lessons and lifecycles that we re-peatedly find ourselves in. Until we are able to fully appreciate a specific "lesson" in our path, *cyclic* be-haviors and results ensue, and in hindsight, we find ourselves trapped in circles of behavior wherein we follow a program of doing the opposite of what we intend to do; pushing away the very energies and forces that we seek to manifest in our life.

All manifestations, forms and variations of energy are part of the same continuum or spectrum. Often times, *cycles* of learning that you find yourself in are a recursive spiral that is only fluid in appearance, carrying consciousness on a figure-8 plane of repeat infinity along spectrums of extremes.

> For example; energetically bouncing between the states of "sadness" and "anger" manifests a continuous state of fluctuation, and therefore frustration or "stress."

VII.

At the level of physical behavior, the motivation – the mobilizing initiative of movement and change – comes from an emotional source. This includes the chemical and hormonal physiologic responses of the body that precede behavior and observable action.

Over time and by validating only what we already believe we know, personal *"reactive patterns"* form from repetition and later come to manifest outwardly seeming as if they are automatic responses: reactive, not proactive.

The concept of being "reactive" versus "proactive" is related frequently in NexGenSys material. When we are thinking and acting "proactively," than we are actively creating and manifesting the life we want in stability by focusing on personal strengths and the things we *can* do to have affect on our *reality*. On the contrary, "reactive" *patterns* lead to mental and behavioral *cycles* that focus on the limitations that other people offer and emphasis on what we *can't* do.

The Human Condition is self-validating. People like to believe that they are in control of their own lives – in control of their *thought patterns* and *behavioral cycles*. In actuality, this process is quite autonomous and requires interaction and programming ahead of time to be effectively in control. Split-second brain firing in the moment draws upon stores of memory and response tendencies that are preexisting.

Someone who is in effect a "self-controlled" person is one who has taught themselves to not "react" rashly or make quick "rash" decisions on impulse. While there is such a thing as "intuition" and being able to sense things outside the normative range of information reception, the type of environmental stimuli and external influence that we regularly encounter in everyday life generally earn "immediate responses" based on programmed knowledge, not true "*gnosis*."

Once you have assimilated specific data and semantics into your 'baseline' or '*belief system*', you will begin to look for and seemingly 'naturally' observe things in the external environment that continuously validate the personal experiences of *reality* that manifest. In essence, what we seek; we find. What we 'process' as experience is all about our "*agreement of reality*."

While these concepts may seem superficial, they are actually some of the most important issues facing a sentient human being operating the Human Condition on the planet earth. This work is primarily the result of years of experimental research and philosophical debate on the problem of why most human behavior is reactive and not creative. This knowledge is critical if you hope to not only comprehend yourself but the people you interact with – and potentially influence the whole...

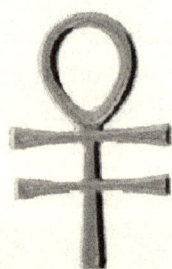

Made in the USA
Las Vegas, NV
28 August 2021